The Black VIrgin

David Arthur Walters

Published by David Arthur Walters, 2024.

THE BLACK VIRGIN

First edition. November 21, 2024.

ISBN: 979-8230749417

Written by David Arthur Walters.

Table of Contents

ISIS - Our Lady of Words

EVERYONE WHO ENJOYS THE RIVER OF LIFE loves a parade in its honor. Wherefore let us tear down our ramshackle houses of discrimination and build a fleet of floats to launch on the flowing floods of time, keeping in mind, as we proceed with our crafts, the mother ship of liberty: the Ark. While at our drafting boards, we shall remember the Argo: she was endowed with a reasoning soul; she was devoted to freedom; she permitted no slaves to board her. Aeschylus said of her, "And tell me where's the sacred beam/That dared the dangerous Euxine stream?"

And, on our way to embarkation, may we sincerely enjoy our procession, as did the Egyptians proceeding to the banks of the Nile to launch their sacred barque or to the temple wherein flowed the sacred Other-World stream whereupon they placed their ark. Yes, let us proceed accordingly, by the while, fearing not The End receding in impenetrable mystery, nor fearing that we shall wind up knowing too much of the arcanum for our own good. True, like After Thought, Epimetheus, we may realize too late that all-gifted Pandora's vase bears goods that turn evil once born into the world; nevertheless, Hope remains in her treasured chest. As Apuleius said of the "Procession of the Savior Goddess" whose "true name" is Isis: "Another carried a box holding secret things and concealing within it the hidden attributes of the sublime faith." Well, the Cornucopia is ideally inexhaustible but, of course, by the goods are found real evils.

In Black Land (Egypt), the Queen of Night was invoked as Isis. In that land Isis was a compassionate conservative compared to Kali in India, where conditions apparently warranted more ruthlessness. Of course Kali, Black Mama, Magic Mother of Maya, merely received what was given to her as destructive thanks for her great creative gift of the Universe to men. Kali wore a necklace of skulls representing the letters of the alphabet; even a moron could become a great poet if he recounted them. By virtue of her maya, The Great Mother, Mahamaya, also appeared in India in an apparently kinder form as Vak, Goddess of Speech, and as Sarasvati, the River Goddess of Eloquence and hence the source of all knowledge and wisdom. But let us return to the goddess of the Nile.

In her black hidden-Moon form, Isis the Black Virgin was the secret inspiration of Light. Although the pure, nude Isis is black, she appears in many colors such as blue-green, red, white, and yellow-gold. As Earth she was the black virginal soil of the Nile, periodically clothed in green garb. She originated in the deepest recesses of Africa, traveling therefrom far and wide. She eventually took the form of a Nubian woman: Nubian women were famous for their beauty, especially in Egypt where Isis staged a stellar performance (her constellation is Virgo), as we can see from her Ten Thousand Names, capitalized to emphasize their archaic propriety:

The Only One, Great Virgin, Mother Egypt, God Mother, Original Mother, Female Ra, Eye of Ra, Green Goddess, Lady of the House of Life, House of Horus, Queen of the Nile, Lady of Tears, Purifier with Water, Creatrix of the Nile Flood, Wife of Inundation, Mother of Stars, Parent of Seasons, Savior of Rich and Poor, Lady of Love, Eternal Throne of Pharaoh, Hidden Goddess of the Underworld, Queen of the Dead, Magician, Healer, Lady of Words of Power, Lady of Breath, Queen of Heaven, Lady of Ten Thousand Names, and so on to infinity beyond the ten thousand heretofore mentionable.

Yet a few more illustrious titles must be mentioned herewith. Isis has been associated with Mary, Lady of Sorrows, or, in Hebrew, Miriam; that is, Sea of Sorrow. In Chaldaic, Miriam is Mistress of the Sea: sailors have called Isis Virgin of the Sea, Stiller of Storms, Pacifier of Gales. Miriam was the sister of Moses (Egyptian: "born" or "son") who was "pulled from the water" (Hebrew: play on the word "Mose"). Moses, like Isis's son Horus, was hidden in a papyrus ark, or nest, near the water. Miriam was also associated with water when she led the singing of praises after the parting of the sea, and also when she died: the life-giving water in the desert dried up.

Isis in her Marianist form is the Ark of the Covenant of the Living Lord; she is the House of the Lord; she is the Immaculate Lady who cannot be spotted in her archetype: but to intentionally defame her is an exposition of misogyny worse than cursing one's own mother.

The original Ark in which the Covenant was deposited contained the secret, perfectly bisexual Name of the Ineffable Creator known only to Mary (in Isis' case, Isis managed to extort the Name of Ra by means of poison, saving him when it was revealed within her). In response to the evocation of the Original Mother, the Name was divided into Two Hands impressed on volcanic tablets—one female, the community, or Bride—the other male, the executor of the laws, or Groom. Upon the tablets were Ten Words of the Fingers of Fire, Seeds of Life, the Perfect Ten who is One—as can be witnessed in the decimal system when 9 is perfected by adding 1 (=10).

Thus the Ark of Isis/Mary was built to carry the Seeds over the waters of chaos, that the Living Law be planted in the Promised Land as her Son, the Decalogue Incarnate. The Ark, cleansed of memory by the baptismal flood waters, served as the Natural Womb of the Son of Man during the perilous voyage from the Other World. Replicas of the fateful, miraculous landing occasionally surface—some of them are made of black basalt; some have been painted with black resin. In other words, black madonnas upholding black sons have been unearthed.

Heretics were murdered for declaring that the black marianic madonnas were images of Isis suckling Horus, the son and avenger of his father Osiris. They were also been burned at the stake for claiming Egyptian magic and religion to be superior to its Christian consequences. Nevertheless, when the old temples and their sites were being whitewashed or demolished, some of the devils to be cast out were overlooked—one even miraculously appeared in a Pope's inner chambers.

Now then, the river or way of Isis is the retinue of living beings proceeding by means of her Ark, the Vessel of Light and Life. Although men replicate her Ark and lay claim to and name their various vessels, the arks are of feminine gender. For example, the Boat of Ra, the Sun-disc Boat of Millions of Years, the Boat to the Other World, are all feminine. Speaking of the Other World, from whence comes Life and whither does it go to return again? From the Other World, personified and directed by Isis, albeit presided over by Osiris (just as Kali the Energy is presided over by the dead Form of her spouse Siva), whom Isis resurrected with her power of breath in order to conceive Horus to avenge the Father who presides over the Other World.

The Secret Chamber, the holy of holies cradling the mystery of human life, is the ark, or womb. From birth to death to birth: what links life to life? The marriage of life and death (the Fates are three, presiding over birth, and death, and the wedding of life and death) the womb is the ark of over the sea of death.

"Ark" is a marvelous and magical word; indeed, a clue to the meaning of arcane, coerce, and exercise: for an ark "contains and maintains, prevents and wards off, pursues and drives out, keeps moving and practices." When we exercise understanding, we coerce chaos: we build containers, categories and concepts, boats of knowledge, ships over seas of distress. Hence an ark is not just a nest, a basket, a box, or a chest; nor is it merely a cave, a coffin, a tomb, or a pyramid. An ark is always a conveyance as well, a chariot through and over and under all the elements to the Beyond. Furthermore, the ark is a space ship bearing time, a time capsule. And a book is an ark, and so are archives and libraries: the banks of the rivers of memory carved out of the elements for future generations are arks of civilization.

Moreover, the soul is the boat of the self on the ocean of spirit. The mind is the ark of light. So is the heart an ark, the ark of love and truth and justice. The house is an ark if it is a home, as is the church housing its infinitesimal portion of the infinite.

But let us not wander too far astray with the Patroness of Navigation, too far to remark that the Island-in-Papyrus-Swamps where Isis conceived Horus and hid him in a nest lest he be murdered, is an ark close to our subject.

During the foregoing parade of terms, several furrowed brows were observed in the crowd. Not everyone was amused or enlightened by the festivities and glowing floats. In fact, certain countenances were waved as flags of contempt, disgust, consternation, and anger. Some remarks were overheard concerning cow-headed freaks and the worship of the Moon, dogs, and crocodiles. Why, one man shouted obscenities as if his own mother had just been vehemently cursed and his father transformed into an impotent cuckold.

Speaking of dogs and crocodiles, a crocodile rising and setting with the Sun was an ark known to the ancient Egyptians as "the fish and seat of Horus, son of Isis." quite naturally, another animal, the sacred cow, never to be eaten, is an ark. As for Isis' Moon, it is the month, the ark or measure of time. Speaking again of dogs, curious dogs helped Isis find a buried child: hence dog-headed Anubis keeps watch over gods just as dogs watch over men.

Nonetheless, setting all that aside, and judging from the epithets (expletives deleted) shouted by the irate man from the crowd, Isis' personal character remains in grave doubt, a doubt that must be addressed.

It is true that Isis, like many of our most prominent forebears, has been the subject of malignant rumors concerning sex and death. The charges were brought long after the facts alleged; if true, the deeds were not considered to be immoral at the time of commission. Furthermore, as civilization supposedly advanced, so went Isis: her stories were brushed up and revised according to current taste, and, when she fell out of favor altogether, she was whitewashed and renamed.

In any event, we are not about to tear up our constitution because of the violence that secured it. Leaving aside the grisly details of her righteous violent moods when exasperated, the acts recounted in the ancient texts assure us that Isis was the very epitome of a chaste and devoted wife and mother. She did not cheat on her husband, nor did she remarry after her death; in fact, she went to the four corners of the earth, risking life and limb, to find him and raise him from the dead. And when, after finding him, he was stolen away by his brother and cut into pieces, she found all the pieces (save the erect vital one) and bound him together again; then she forgave the perpetrator. Nowhere in the wide world could be found another such a persevering, courageous, compassionate, and merciful woman! No son of man, having heard of her sorrows over her sick child and how she saved him could want a better mother. Her ancient promise to her son was inscribed on a stele found Alexandria:

"I will protect thee, O my son. Fear thou not, O son, my glorious one. No evil thing whatsoever shall happen unto thee, for in thee is the seed whereof things which are to be shall be created." And furthermore, "No reptile that stingeth shall have the mastery over thee, and no lion shall crush thee or gain mastery over thee. Thou art the son of the holy god."

Apuleius said of Isis, many year later, "Thou art in truth the eternal and holy savior of the human race, beneficent in helping mortal men, and thou bringest the sweet love of a mother to the trials of the unfortunate."

Isis was not, as a rude Byzantine iconoclast said disparagingly of her Western form, a purse to be used for deposits and then cast aside once the investment matured. For Isis, because of her undying love, had the gift of the healing power of wisdom. She was called the Daughter of Wisdom, for her mentor Thoth was father of Wisdom. Observing her love and sorrow for her poisoned child, Thoth gave Isis the healing power with the guarantee it would work in all like cases. An ancient stele mentions another case, that of a noble woman's child stung by a deadly scorpion because the woman refused to help Isis:

"Mine own heart was sad," said Isis, "for the child's sake, and I wished to restore to life him that had committed no fault. O poison of Tefen, come forth, and appear on the ground; come not in, approach not, for I am Isis the goddess, and I am the Lady of Words of Power, and I know how to work with the words of power, and most mighty are my words! O all ye reptiles which sting, hearken unto me, and fall ye down on the ground!" Isis applied her hands to the stricken child—mention was also made of the use of barley and an herb—and the child was saved from certain death. So by the exercise of her powerful method, the saving ark of words and technique, she coerced evil and staved off death.

Furthermore, because of the resurrecting power of her breath, Isis was called the Lady of Immaculate Conception: she raised the father from the Other World to conceive the son in this one. And, as mother's milk saves the child from death once resurrected, so do her words save him from death due to ignorance while living in this world. Therefore, Isis' civilizing inventions were legion: for example, the arts of writing, healing, spinning, brewing, bread making, sailing, and irrigation. Her agricultural achievements, by the way, allowed Osiris to abolish cannibalism; that is to say, the eating of animals including man, the most divine one, at least as far as her shaven-headed intimate were concerned.

Our resume parading Isis' virtues would be inadequate if we failed to respond to the serious allegations questioning her conceptual virginity. Indeed, we have heard from the crowd a rebuttal against the virginity proposition, indicating a contradiction that, once made obvious, would supposedly wreck even the faith of a devout fool, if only he were mentally competent enough to entertain it: to wit, that the mother of all living beings cannot be, at the same time, a virgin. It is said that such a woman would a dissolute slovenly slut rather than an absolutely virtuous woman. Our response to the defamation may be as rambling as the Nile or as convoluted as the magic serpent of Isis. Nonetheless, we must respond confidently and at some length; after all, logical contradictions are not necessarily fatal, agonizing as they may be: we see their synthesis in marriage persisting everywhere despite all arguments to the contrary.

Yes, we have heard the ancient rumor that nary a virgin could be found in all of ancient Egypt. But that aspersion is as profane and vulgar as the rumors of orgies associated with Isis' festivities. The wiser perspective must be employed here; and, as we know, wisdom is little known, especially the esoteric wisdom that defies common sense. The initiates of the occult cult of Isis knew well the fecund secret of carnal knowledge: more expressly, that what is forbidden and kept secret excites the passions enormously. That is to say, the virginity of Isis is occluded precisely for some very productive reasons, causes, and becauses. Her veil of vulgar illusions conceal the prized purity of her grail; her seemingly impossible perfection is the original motive of the desire always falling short of her underskirts.

Eternal Isis came before all men and women born of her; thus she, Universal Mother, is unspotted by vulgar precedent and is, therefore, unimpeachable except by those who hate life and love death; even so, Isis would comfort those who regret the day they were born, forgiving their ignorant contumely. Therefore all impeachments fail to convict the Lady Of Mercy who takes precedent over everything within her ark and thus presides over the fairest trial or all.

Perhaps our abstract grammatical intercourse should be more concretely embellished by reference to the intercourse of the Nile with its Ground on the river bed. Consider the black virgin soil embracing the Nile, a strip of fertile earth broadening as it approaches the delta. The river depositing its alluvium is sometimes alluded to as Osiris, black god of the Other World and father of this green one, who periodically appears as the dragon flood subdued by Isis. The dragon rises and falls in cadence with her joys and sorrows. Her tears flood the canal of life with the fertile silt of love lost upriver. After the waters break, fall and recede into the earth, Isis rejoices in her offspring Horus, inspiring him with her power of breath. Horus comes to "avenge" Osiris, his father who is back at work in the Other World. Therefore is Earth given renewed life.

We must note here that the ancient Egyptian theologians, in their trinitarian efforts to reconcile unity with diversity, to explain how there can be two yet only one, or how two can come from one or become one, sometimes resorted to speculative hermaphroditism. Nevertheless, their highest god, being therefore omnipotent, had no difficulty conceiving without the benefit of opposite sexes and logical proofs. In any event, the self-fertilizing Nile matrix was their primary guide, male or female or both, their self-ruling or autarkical archetype, wherein was concealed the unity of the cosmic trinity: cause-force-effect, or mother-father child, who are one because no one is conceivable without the other two. But the Universal Mother, when the unity is divided, has virginal priority and is actually the unifying principle between the father and the child.

Furthermore, the extrapolation of the holy nuclear family, the familial triangle, is accomplished by means of royal incest: another explanation for the original production of population is implausible. We are still, loosely speaking, engaged in incest; for the virtues of human progression, incest was technically limited to the Royal Circle, where the centralizing force was conserved as life branched out from the Big Bang like rays from the sun disc. In the Royal Circle, the Virgin Universal Mother is the mother of her father who is her brother and her husband as well as her son. She is the perfect circle of family relations. She is the Virgin of Immaculate Conception because she alone gave birth to the first man. The Universal Mother, when unity is divided, still has priority.

Speaking abstractly on behalf the iconoclasts who adore Isis untouched, no physical image or metaphysical concept of Isis does her purity justice: any factual or ideal representation is therefore blasphemous, even the most pleasing portrait of Madonna.

Metaphorically speaking, the mystical Isis is analogous to the absolute, continuous space that goes on forever and ever uninterrupted, a void pregnant with every possibility. That space has a real meaning although nobody knows just what it is. It is the absolute space of "common" sense, analogous to divine presence, the "empty" space metaphysicians and physicists regard as existentially untenable and conceptually impossible after imbibing great draughts of befuddling formulae from her breast. Isis, in that non-sense, is absolute liberty at the root of matter, mother of mass by virtue of her inertial matrix. Crudely speaking, it is as if something comes from nothing, that nothing being therefore the "container" or ark of All. As boundless as continuous "empty" space may be, we still imagine space as feminine: she is the most voluptuous of females because of her infinite virginity. In her each man has his virgin to cultivate, his virgin plot of soil by the Nile, and she is as good as any and as good as all: she is a model of perfection, for no two objects can occupy the same portion of her at the same time, yet she occupies or contains them wherever and whenever they may be in the wherever/whenever continuum.

Now then, as we have been making the virginity of Isis perfectly clear, the Sun of her Maya is about to set upon our parade.

Nevertheless, we shall proceed gaily into the festivities of the Night, for only there may the black virginal beauty of Isis be truly intuited.

Primitive Vestiges and Anal Therapy

The Psychological Implications of Elephant Dung

IF WE ARE TO TOLERATE the vestiges of "primitive" religions represented by The Holy Virgin Mary, then, in order to keep our conscience clean, we should give some brief regard to the post-modern psychoanalytic return to the Primitive, at least in reference to elephant dung and associated matters. We therefore note a reference to elephant dung by French psychoanalyst Jacques Lacan.

According to Sherry Turkle in her book *Psychoanalytic Politics*, Lacan raised the elephant dung issue before a MIT audience in 1975. He said he was reasonably certain in his capacity as an analyst that man does have an interior: the evidence he found for that interior was the presence of excrement. Lacan claimed that man is the only animal who does not instinctively know what to do with his dung, except the dog, who is also civilized and is therefore also dung-encumbered. Lacan said that elephant dung does not occupy much space even though it is reasonable to expect it to require, considering the size of the animal producing it, enormous accommodations. Then he equated civilization with excrement. He remarked that it would take a long time for people to understand what he was talking about. His audience thought he was delirious and senile - he was 72 at the time.

Lacan must not have been familiar with the production capacity of elephants. Thai researchers have recently generated electricity from elephant-dung natural gas. An elephant produces 88-110 lbs. of dung per day, enough to produce cooking gas for a family of three, or it can be used as feedstock for an electric generator. But the cost is not cheap. The minimum price of construction of a fermentation pit, pipeline and storage tank is around $800 and a generator that could use the gas costs around $2,667. The Thai ministry responsible for the project plans to release a report promoting use of the method nationwide, especially in the North and the Northeast where most of the country's domesticated elephants are found and the problem of how to dispose of the elephants' waste is most acute. -(AP)- Bangkok, Thailand, February 23, 2000.

Despite that contradiction to Lacan's hypothesis, to be fair we shall render a few extractions from the ancient literature in his support or his general position. Take, for instance, sacred elephant dung.

Elephants themselves have long been associated with divinity and wisdom. The elephant is the Indian dragon with the snake of wisdom for its proboscis. It is the great god Indra's indispensable steed or vehicle, called Airavata, one of his necessary auspicious signs, equally important if not more so than his chakra, jewel, queen, treasure and horse. Airavata. meaning "produced from the ocean", came from the Ocean of Milk stirred up at the Creation. He is a cloud-white or milky-white elephant. Wherefore wars were once waged for the mere possession of a white elephant, and their images were placed as capitals on pillars and worshiped.

Celestial elephants have wings and can fly like clouds. It has long been known that they, as does the Chinese dragon, bring luck and abundance down to Earth. In fact, elephants fertilize the Earth Goddess: therefore she loves the sound of approaching elephants. Furthermore, so powerful is the fresh dung of white elephants that an ancient prescription for barrenness provides that infertile women stand in it for one hour prior to intercourse with their husbands.

Moreover, since the elephant is a royal vehicle, elephant dung may be a sign of the coming of a great lord. For instance, consider the myth about the birth of Buddha. His mother, Mayadevi, fell asleep and dreamed. Bodhisattva, in the form of a white elephant descended from a golden mountain, circled her bed clockwise three times, smote her right side, then entered her womb. A Brahmin, upon hearing her account , prognosticated, "Thou shalt have a son. If he dwells in the house he will become a king, a universal monarch if he leaves the house and goes forth from the world, he will become a Buddha, a remover in the world of the veil of ignorance."

Incidentally, lest we become to grave about this matter, The Mesopotamians had a sense of humor concerning the droppings of the great elephant: their account of the Flood relates how the elephants stood on one side of the Ark, nearly causing it to roll over and capsize by weight of their excretions.

That example alone should suffice to support Dr. Lacan's statement asserting the positive relation of dung to the advance of civilization. Nonetheless, a few more references will reinforce our case. Take for instance, the first anthropological evidence of capitalism: it seems a primitive North American tribe gorged themselves to speed up their production of ordure, then baked it in the sun and stored it for future consumption in case of dire need.

Also consider the fact that, among the Kujamaat Diola of Senegal, certain individuals used to defecate in secret places in the bushes, then adopted the leavings as their personal totems or animated doubles. And note that an Africa sacred object might be worthless in itself: it is merely the means of communication. For a descendant of Nigerian elephant hunters, that object might very well be a clump of shellacked elephant dung, a symbol of power intended to wish happy elephant hunting as well as the capture of many erotic butterflies by the illustrious sons of "The Holy Virgin Mary."

Mind you that which is called "primitive" is not as primitive as it sometimes seems when we proceed to analyze it, hence we return to postmodern excremental psycho-anal-ysis in hopes we may obtain good therapy during our excremental discourse. The evolution of dung-consciousness in the developing child must be mentioned in our context. According to the psycho-anal lore, a child becomes intensely interested in its productions during the anal stage. According to the founding fathers of psychoanalysis, the child exchanges the wet, stinky and sticky product for clean dry sand, although he might pour water in the sand or show a predilection for mud. That product is, in turn, traded for pebbles, rocks and marbles. Hard currency, jewels and precious metals might eventually follow. If a man has been raised properly, he will not want to touch dirty money: liquid currency is disgusting to him. Working capital must not be held in the form of cash in pocket or in bank accounts but must be fully vested in productive assets. A hygienically inclined man will prefer plastic cards, and have his digital statements handled by his accountants. However, he might often be involved in construction projects that leave petrified dejecta all over the land, such as buildings, roads, machines and other stools of power.

Several sorts of characters might emerge because of the different quirks of toilet training. A child might become an artist. Every true artist is a sort of rebel. The rebellious child might start his first savings account during the training process just to give himself the pleasure of squandering it as he pleases despite the best efforts of his parents. However, he might scorn savings altogether because his parents cherish the same.

On the other hand, because of some other accident of upbringing during the critical anal stage, a child might become an uptight tightwad, a constipated person who might know he belongs in analysis but does not want to pay for it; by the way, the Greek word for analysis means "to loosen up." Postmodern excremental therapy is required. We have by no means exhausted the prospects of civilization and its discontents relative to the anal erogenous zone. Yet we can have comfort in knowing that the latest group therapy practice may provide a great deal of relief to the malcontents and the discontented. Two hour sessions are conducted while the group sits on toilets; the pioneering analyst got this idea from the customary practice of men in ancient Rome who sat for hours on public toilets chatting with each other while taking care of business. Naturally, this new anal therapy is being subsidized by the United States Government.

Indeed! The Surgeon General of the United States has defined mental illness as a mental state interfering with production and relationships. A man must achieve optimum productivity in our society in order to have fully productive relationships, yet his duty to consume and to maximize production may interfere with those relations. In any event, a healthy individual must make at least an adequate or "normal" contribution to the Gross National Product. Consumerism is the official state religion: continuous production is worshiped because of the manna that products supposedly contain, and because of the cathartic release of tension. Therefore the new anal therapy is conducive to the religion of consumption and productive, and therefore merits the allocation of public funds.

So Mr. Lacan might not be so crazy and coprophilic as he seemed when he said civilization is excremental. Of course, he employs a figure of speech which apparently accounts for a massive sublimation of a primitive movement. I opine we are going overboard: a great deal of crap is now being frantically produced in developed countries just so people can get a bite to eat.

The Black Virgin in Brooklyn

THE CONTROVERSIAL 'SENSATION' Exhibit at the Brooklyn museum of Art on October 2, 1999, received sensational responses from the public: law suits were filed; dung was hurled; the public vomited; iconoclasm was attempted.

The Holy Virgin Mary painted by Chris Ofili, a young British artist of Nigerian descent, was the epicenter of the cultural upheaval. The image portrays a black woman decorated with some shellacked elephant dung the artist claims is symbolic of his African heritage. An odd assortment of female buttocks clipped from pornographic magazines flits about her head like butterflies.

"Sensation" attracted a curious crowd to the museum. However, based on what was seen and heard in the media, most people would not have given a farthing to see the show. Nonetheless, the symbolic elements of the controversy are invaluable and could, if taken advantage of, work a transformation of dung into gold or of foolishness into the wisdom it presently occludes.

For instance, if the subject of *The Holy Virgin Mary* is the esoteric Black Virgin who presides over the Underground Stream flowing in its spiral course throughout the Hidden Church, then her apparition, perhaps unwittingly made manifest by Mr. Ofili, presages events of biblical proportion.

According to occult tradition, the Black Virgin's appearance precedes a carnival of feminine equality and liberation. A poor compassionate woman shall commune there with mankind, and from the virginal black earth shall emerge a son who shall reveal the Secret Doctrine in the chasm of his poetic ambiguities: those who seek the Grail in the gap shall behold the face of Mother Night on the threshold of bliss.

The Black Virgin prophecy appertains to the long-awaited liberation of man's feminine side from the violent patriarchal oppression of his forefathers, and to the ensuing procession of the Matriarchal Age of Love. Some thinkers now believe that women are almost liberated. However, they expect a male backlash rather than a love fest to follow. They opine postmodern man has been so badly whipped by modern feminism that he has lost his sublime sense of ultimate male utility; that is, his identification with some higher purpose than becoming, for example, an Internet or Wall Street whiz, movie star, or sports idol. Hence he is expected to strike out violently in a last-ditch effort to erect his self-dignity.

Nonetheless, we find nothing new in postmodern man's misogyny, psychological weakness, and reliance on brute force to redeem himself:it would be a classic mistake to blame his typical behavior on the current Women's Movement.

Fortunately, however, for all those concerned, women are experts in the struggle for personal identity, wherefore they have much to contribute to the male struggle, just as the long struggle of slaves for their freedom helps to emancipate all men. Yes, indeed, perhaps feminist expertise may be the key to the mysterious evolution of sexual peace. Wherefore, when the prophecy is fulfilled, man shall come to equal terms and merge with the real woman fully exposed: the War Between the Sexes shall end in bliss.

In the interim, at least until the peace treaty is signed, the Black Virgin, the gap between the father and the son, must somehow be whitewashed.

A week before Christmas, Mr. Heiner, a 72-year old retired teacher, feigned sickness, slipped behind the Plexiglas barrier. and smeared white paint on *The Holy Virgin Mary,* because he and his wife believed the image was "blasphemous." A museum spokesperson called his act "incomprehensible," and the vandal was charged with felony criminal mischief.

The painting was promptly cleaned and re-displayed. But elsewhere the whitewash has had centuries to dry: the ideal mother resides unspotted in her candle-lit niche, a glowing ornament to emasculated virtue, yet a real source of confusion to men still in full possession of their senses. Her retinue of ideal ladies-in-waiting are legion: one, and sometimes more, for each man. She is the lost mother each man seeks in his wife; she is the first housekeeper or oekonomikus; she is the principle of propriety on a pedestal; she is the trustee of native identity; she is prime productive private property. And she is much more than all that: she bears a burden beyond man's comprehension, laboring where he is incompetent to the task.

But let us return to Brooklyn and the case of dung in hand. Some time after Mr. Heiner smeared white paint on the detested image inside, another man outside doused the museum with red paint for unknown reasons. Yet another protester hurled dung at the museum. Moreover, 200 New Yorkers assembled in Manhattan's Washington Square Park, paid a dollar each to don a latex glove, and hurl dung at a portrait of Mayor Rudolph Giuliani. who was depicted as the Madonna. Reporters later reported that the police raided the apartment of one Stephen Powers, a graffiti artist who disclosed on a radio talk show that he was responsible for staging the protest. A great deal of material was seized, including an antique set of brass knuckles hanging on his wall: Mr. Powers was arrested and charged with the criminal possession of a weapon. Joey Skaggs, the man who actually designed the mayor's portrait, was barely mentioned in the reports.

The dishonored mayor, characterized by his liberal foes as an anal-retentive conservative, wanted to halt the museum's funding, cut off its utilities, and evict it from the public facilities. He denounced the exhibit as "sick". He was eventually overruled by Judge Nina Gershon, who held that the mayor and the city were threatening the neutrality required of government in the sphere of religion.

So far none of this is very astonishing in a city where horses are forced by the city to wear diapers and where pooper-scoopers are a common appliance. Nor is it surprising that the 'Sensation' exhibit included, much to the horror of animal rights activists, dismembered animals in large containers of formaldehyde.

Now then, as we can see in the symbolic context, Mr. Ofili's intentions were irrelevant when he created the image *The Holy Virgin Mary* we have so conveniently appropriated for our various excursive interpretations. If the artist had malice in his heart, his heart will surely suffer. Nevertheless, a few pious folks in Brooklyn are probably burning candles, making mysterious signs in thin air, kneeling and saying special prayers before a facsimile of his work; perhaps a photo clipped from the catalog or the newspaper. Shall we charge them with bad taste, or with idolatry?

Some sympathetic souls believe a little superstitious ignorance might be healthy for vulgar people despite our own noble aesthetic and religious convictions. In any event, no matter what our perspectives and prejudices might be, we should thank Mr. Ofili and his ilk for playing their roles, that we may play ours.

We should also thank Mayor Rudolph Giuliani for his intolerance and his vigorous litigious opposition to "Sensation" The mayor plays the part of a character many generous liberals love to hate: that of an orderly, parsimonious and obstinate mayor sitting on the throne of Babylon under which he is occasionally self-moved to deposit in a box his various execrations in the form of regulatory commandments. Liberals rarely receive mercy under his tarnished seat of power, which doubles as a ceiling to all below. Liberals can only hope his angels will fly him and his portable throne elsewhere. Be that as it may, wherever his seat of power may move him, his inhospitality towards the Black Virgin during her visit to Brooklyn has only served to further illustrate the enormous power she holds, even over the most powerful men.

The Black Virgin in Egypt

THE DUNG AFFIXED by Chris Ofili to his *The Holy Virgin Mary* had sensational effects all over the world, where people familiar with dung discussed its vices and virtues. Although mothers are familiar with dung no matter whether they live in town or country, city fathers who do not change diapers are reluctant to have much to do with it personally, assigning such matters to their wives and other sanitation officials. Of course, farmers with livestock and those who use natural methods of cultivation are intimate with dung.

The mention of dung is certainly appropriate within the historical context of *The Holy Virgin Mary* scandal. Hebrew prophets were well aware of the fertilizing property of dung whether real or ideal: they called idols "dung" - all idols were dung except their own ark and its deposits.

The Egyptians, whose sacred images were referred to as dung by the Hebrews, had good reason to appreciate the virtues of dung. They used dung as fertilizer to supplement the silt carried down to them by the Nile. Therefore, if we are to trace the Black Virgin's movements about the world, it would behoove us to examine the dung issue in Egypt.

First of all, the Black Virgin was know as Isis in Egypt. Isis was the Queen of all domains. She was understandably most popular as Goddess of the Nile; her great river, sometimes known as her husband, Osiris, flowed through her black virgin soil, much to the benefit of mankind: in Isis' heyday, her black virgin soil provided a living paradise on Earth. Osiris himself came and went; he was associated with the Underground Stream as god of the Other World, returning through his son Horus; but Isis was the First Mother and the Eternal Throne of Osiris.

The ancient Egyptians were expert irrigation-canal builders, and of course they were familiar with the fertilizing virtues of dung. Although a great deal has changed since the good old days, especially in respect to religion, dung is to this very day known in Egypt for its ancient virtue as a fertilizer; that clue to the travels of the Black Virgin beckons us to take advantage of an optional tour of the Nile - not quite the pretty cruise offered by the travel agencies.

Since the Nile has been damned at Aswan to tame the flood in order to curb the broad feast-or-famine swings resulting from the natural cycle, chemical fertilizers must be employed, for there is insufficient dung to make up for the lost silt. Critics of the Aswan High Dam complain of the lack of nutrients in the soil. They also claim that the silt-free water erodes barrages and bridge foundations, that it has caused coastal erosion of the delta, and that the reduction of flows has caused saline inundation from the Mediterranean resulting not only in the salty soil but also the loss of fish.

Furthermore, the artificial lake behind the Aswan dam has submerged and threatens to further submerge the ancient artifacts of one of the first organized states in human history, Nubia, and has run the Nubians, a black people who once ruled Egypt for over a century, off their land. Nubian women were famed for their beauty, an ideal beauty employed by artists as the model for certain black granite statues of Isis. Ironically and fortunately, the great temple of Isis at Philae in Nubia was removed to the island of Agilkia. The cult of Isis survived in Nubia to about the 6th century, long after she had been remodeled into a white virgin in Europe. Other monuments in Nubia have not been nor will they be so lucky. In fact, it seems Nubia has lost her attraction. Some Nubians now long for those ancient days, such as the day when the legendary Moses married a Nubian much to the dismay of his sister Miriam, the prophetess; perhaps not because Miriam was a racist, but because the Kushite woman was a prophetess of Isis in direct competition with Miriam's own practice.

Yes, excremental side excursions can serve as food for thought and fertilizer for future growth. But let us remain in Egypt for a bit longer and travel back in time to the carnival, to the procession of shrines, accompanied by flutes, tambourines, hand-clapping, dancing, singing, and, amongst many other things, to generous offerings of wine, beer, oil and milk—yet a vase of water takes precedence, whether it anoints the fore or aft of the precious ark. And here comes yet another ark, of Isis, bearing her king, who prays the prayer of all kings, for a single blessing: Eternal Life.

The sacred casket of Isis' consort Osiris is borne, on long staves passing through metal rings, by twelve black-cassocked disciples led by their pope. The pontiff wears the garment and carries the magic club of the first world hero, then prehistoric Hercules, the heroic Cave Man of the Stone Age who cleared the Way for civilization.

Every significant personage in our parade has his float staffed by a crew of priests and their pontiff. And what wonderful conveyances the floats are, over land, sea, and sky. We enjoy the fragrant beauty of the talented women everywhere to be seen, some of whose charms exceed the excellencies of Elizabeth Taylor in her Egyptian garb, eyes protected by blue eye-shadow.

But hold on: what is that "thing" in the boat over there? That beetle with hawk-wings pushing a ball of fresh dung before it? That beetle protected by the enveloping wings of two angels, Inspiration and Expiration, fanning the breath of Truth? That thing is Khepri, the dung-beetle form of the Sun-god creator, represented by a scarab emblem wherever life is expected to go on despite its travails and its seemingly final tragic conclusion.

Khepri is reputedly even older than the great Ra-form of the Sun-god. Khepri is the sunrise, the morning, the birth of a new day, the resurrection of the body. He is, therefore, very good news. The scarab beetle lays its egg in dung and then pushes it around until it becomes a ball from which the larva eventually emerges. The wet and warm ark of dung pushed around by the beetle was, to the Egyptians, analogous to the Sun pushed around the sky by a huge beetle.

But we must bring our option tour to a screeching halt. Even in its brevity, our brief excursus into the excremental culture of Egypt reveals that dung is not something to be scorned and set aside as obscene, disgusting and useless, but it is rather something to be examined for its highest and best uses, a material to be pushed ahead as our own globe hurtles at an astonishing relative speed through black virgin space. Even though he might have been unconscious of his motive, perhaps that is why Chris Ofili shellacked a clump of dung on his painting 'The Holy Virgin Mary.' We should keep that in mind during our future excursions into excremental culture.

Smashing the Barriers of Love

The elephant dung affixed upon 'The Holy Virgin Mary', an allegedly blasphemous image of the Madonna created by Chris Offili, a British artist, and exhibited at the Brooklyn Museum of Art on October 2, 1999, resulted in an indignant uproar throughout the city and nation. Mr. Ofili's allusion to his African heritage as the inspiration for the excremental adornment did not satisfy the caustic conservative critics who demanded the immediate removal of the insult and the withdrawal of public funding for the museum.

Critics who believed the image was desecrated by the dung necessarily believed the image was otherwise sacred, wherefore they were idolaters themselves, for images of beings are not the beings themselves. Indeed, staunch mystics have traditionally averred that any figurative representation whatsoever of the only possible Holy One, no matter how lovely the image might be, is sacrilegious. The Divine Mother is Immaculate Space, the Maternal Ark of All, the Dark Womb, the Black Virgin.

Iconomachists, people who hate the worship of images, would normally have been too busy waging war on Catholic images to be concerned with a single image at the Brooklyn Museum. In any case, people who love images are better idolaters than those who hate them. The squabble between the two idolatrous camps might be called a dung fight. Indeed, the Greek word eidolon is used to translate the Hebrew word for dung – Ezekiel's favorite term for idol was gillotim, meaning "dunghill". That is to say, idols are worthless vanities or nothing at all, as are fixed ideas carved on stone or written in books and worshiped as such.

For example, posting the Decalogue on the wall to be adored as some sort of magic charm or formula is absurd. The Ten Commandments should be discussed for a few minutes everyday, until the spirit in which they were uttered is circumscribes the hearts of every participant in the great conversation. That conversation must not end in stone, for such a stone would mark the grave site of human civilization, which is, after all, morally and mentally – that is to say spiritually – inspired.

No, the ultimate sacred power cannot be confined to an idol in a certain location, not even in the Ark of the Covenant in Jerusalem; as Jeremiah said:

"I will give you shepherds after my own heart, and these shall feed you on knowledge and discretion. And when you have increased and become many in the land, then – it's Yahweh who speaks – no one will ever say again: Where is the ark of the covenant of Yahweh? There will be no thought of it, no memory of it, no regret for it, no making of another. When that time comes, Jerusalem shall be called The Throne of Yahweh; all the nations will gather there in the name of Yahweh and will no longer follow the dictates of their own stubborn hearts." (The Jerusalem Bible).

Jeremiah took a dim view of things in his day (c.640-580 BCE). He wished he had not been born. He prayed for the death of his family. He shunned society and avoided marriage. He thought his god Yahweh had raped him. He was a traitor to his country. He believed it was Yahweh's will for Judah to submit to the Babylonians; surrender would be "the way of life", and resistance "the way of death," yet he turned down a handsome offer from Babylon. He was eventually carried off by his people to Egypt, where he was presumably stoned to death. In contrast to his pessimistic outlook, Jeremiah had a bright place in mind for his people, a utopian dream city, a dream city that was never realized on Earth.

Although he may have been mistaken about the virtues of a dream city, Jeremiah spoke with the authority of personal experience, if not from divine revelation, about arks and political reform. He was born when the great iconoclast King Josiah was elevated, at 8 years of age, to the throne of Judah, by the revolutionary faction after the assassination of King Amon. Judah had been a vassal of the Assyrian Empire, which had imposed its alien cults; but the Empire had weakened, and fell into chaos. Egypt was also weak at the time, hence Judah was presented with a golden opportunity, and Josiah happened to be king at the right place and right time for reformation, and he acted accordingly. Now Jeremiah commended Josiah for being a just and righteous King; Jeremiah might have been an itinerant preacher of Josiah's reforms in the early days; even so, he was greatly disillusioned.

During repairs to the Temple, whose cult and priests Jeremiah sharply criticized, the Deuteronomy book, purportedly the record of farewell address delivered by Moses on the verge of the Promised Land, was found and brought to Josiah. Deuteronomy contains a revised covenant or treaty between Yahweh and His vassal, Israel. Josiah was so taken aback when he read it that he rent his garments and proceeded with the reformation forthwith. The Deuteronomy we have today is not what it was then, but the gist of the old text is apparent in the new, and one legal clause of the code is particularly striking:

"You must destroy completely all the places where the nations you dispossess have served their gods, on high mountains, on hills, under any spreading tree; you must tear down their altars, smash their pillars, cut down their sacred poles, set fire to the carved images of their gods and wipe out their name from that place.

That injunction was even more severe than the proclamation of Ikhnaton, the sun-worshiping, monotheistic pharaoh who ordered the obliteration of all inscribed references to plural "gods." Ikhnaton, after all, had a trinity-in-Aton, and he was obliged to tolerate some of the lesser, more popular personifications, particularly those enjoyed by the populace in the privacy of their abodes. But Yahweh was not as tolerant as the legendary Pharaoh of Love, at least not according to Mosaic lore. Yahweh made only one exception to absolute iconoclasm:

"Not so are you to behave towards Yahweh your God. You must seek Yahweh your God only in the place he himself will choose from among all your tribes, to set down His name there and give it a home. There you shall bring your sacrifices, tithes, and offerings."

That commandment dovetailed nicely with Josiah's agenda: the centralization of government and worship in Jerusalem. It was an agenda both religious and political. People did have to draw nice distinctions between religion and politics in those days. Religion was about power, and politics was about who had it. The early monarch was the penultimate if not ultimate personification of power for his people, whether he was an agent of god or was presumed to be a god himself, hence the modern argument over whether ancient iconoclasm was religiously or politically motivated does not coincide with the nature of the beast. Like David, Josiah was anointed by Yahweh. Like Moses, he was leading his people to freedom. He was the instrument of Yahweh's law. Obedience to that law would save Israel, Yahweh's chosen people, from bondage to despised foreign and local enemies.

Josiah's people went on a rampage, smashing and burning the shrines and idols of the enemy. The discrimination was justified because only Israel had a valid contract with Yahweh: Canaanites, Moabites, Ammonites, members of the reviled ruling class and others had no absolute right to exist in Yahweh's domain. Although the Hebrew Lord was a loving god whose affection extended even to birds, trees, and oxen, he was also a jealous landlord who must not be provoked. Even the local shrines to Yahweh were abolished, their priests ousted or slain; there was only one temple good enough for Yahweh: the Temple of Jerusalem. And at one curtained, windowless end of the Temple was placed the Ark of the Covenant of the Lord, the receptacle of the true Yahweh legislation, the central symbol of Josiah's administration in the name of Yahweh, the very throne or stool of god. The idolatrous cult of the ark, perfected by ancient Egyptians and Hebrews, was derived from prehistoric Black Africa, where even today a sacred stool is covered, carried in procession, and then re-lodged in a holy chamber on one end of the lodge, where the holy stool – standing for the law excreted by divinity – and its occupant, now invisible to the public, are protected by spirits and privileged attendants.

All priests and prophets were now under Josiah's control; the former political authority of local priests was vested in his provincial magistrates. As the revenue flowed into Jerusalem, King Josiah sought to centralize and strengthen his army, and to extend his territory. He decided to engage in battle the forces of Pharaoh "Necho", who was on his way to help Assyria against Babylonia. Josiah believed that if he were to defeat Necho's forces, he could unite Judah with Israel. But Josiah was slain: Assyria was defeated; the Egyptians withdrew; Israel was forced to submit to Babylonia, the New Mesopotamian Empire.

As in the case of Ikhnaton, Josiah's reforms died with him: the old idols and high places were soon restored; Jerusalem and its fine Temple were eventually destroyed. Jeremiah had in fact prophesied the Temple's destruction, denouncing the people's dependence on it.

Thus do we have an instructive historical occasion of iconoclasm to reflect upon after considering the dung-laden image of a contemporary artist, an artist of African heritage for whom dung may or may not have been sacred in itself, or perhaps made sacrosanct by slapping it on his Madonna along with what appears to be vaginal butterflies – incidentally, elephant dung, particularly the dung of a white elephant, has long been considered to have magical properties in certain parts of the world. As indignant critics wage war over our postmodern excremental culture instead of loving their enemies as their religion professes, we might try to match our deeds with the admittedly absurd command to love our neighbors – the command exists because we hate them.

Why not lovingly smash all the symbolic barriers between us? It is said that Ikhnaton's religion of iconoclastic love failed because he did not resort to arms to enforce it – as for loving his neighbors, he did not send material aid to his besieged allies. Certain archaeologists now claim – based on the evidence of well-worn footpaths of many soldiers tramping along the perimeter of Amarna – that Ikhnaton's new capital for loving the Power-in-the-Disc was in fact a paranoid armed circle.

As for the commandments to love and fear a transcendental lord as sufficient incentive to desist from our crimes against humanity, faith in words alone shall not suffice to accomplish the works. In Josiah's case, we see that words in a box, even when supported by the force of arms, do not suffice for enduring, radical reform, for such reform must be of the willing heart.

Ikhnaton

The ultimate sacred power cannot be arbitrarily confined to an idol tangible or intangible, nor can it be encompassed by the city of a god such as the utopian dream city Jeremiah had in mind instead of the real Jerusalem he was confronted with. No, a thoroughgoing iconoclast would eschew the worship of a city, even if it were the throne of a god or a central seat of power. Indeed, desert prophets often condemned cities for being race-mixing whores. Iconoclasts would fain destroy any worshiped object—not only a carved idol, painted image, and such, but an entire city. For instance, the dream city built by the iconoclastic pharaoh Ikhnaton (He-who-serves-Aton) during the end of Egypt's Eighteenth Dynasty: he named his city Ikhnaton, or City of the Horizon of the Sun-disk.

Ikhnaton found the site for his holy city in the middle of nowhere, in the black virgin soil undefiled by the pantheon of gods that Egypt had accumulated over the centuries: "For it was Aton, my Father, that brought me to this City of the Horizon. There was not a noble who directed me to it. There was not any man in the whole land who led me to it, saying, 'It is fitting for his majesty that he make a City of the Horizon of Aton in this place'...Behold the Pharaoh found that this site belonged not to a prince, nor to a princess. There was no right for any man to act as owner of it."

So it was there that Ikhnaton built his ark, a city to carry the seeds of the revolutionary race consecrated to the Sun-god. He built it quickly of brick and mortar along modern, "natural" lines—there was no time for massive quarrying—and inscribed on a stone tablet his vow never to leave it: "I will not pass beyond it...for ever and ever," he promised. His oath and the tablet upon which it was written would forever endure, he declared: "It shall not be erased. It shall not be washed out. It shall not be kicked. It shall not be struck with stones." This is particularly ironic in view of the fact that the city only flourished for about twenty-five years: it was razed to the ground after his death. In any case, never before had a king built a city so thoroughly suited to the worship of one god.

Ikhnaton was portrayed with an oddly shaped head, a thin face with a brooding, in-drawn expression, a slender neck, narrow sloping shoulders, protruding breasts, a pot-belly and wide hips. He apparently wore simple clothing and did not adorn himself with jewelry: his personal distinctions were caricatured and copied by the naturalistic art of the day—he was flattered as the model of natural beauty to be imitated. Ikhnaton's unusual conduct is the subject of endless speculation. He has been variously described as an introspective intellectual, an iconoclast, revolutionary, idealist and modernist, as well as an hallucinating mystic and an hermaphrodite. Given the incest noted by travelers to Egypt, he may have been the model for Sophocles' Oedipus. A far-fetched theory opines that Ikhnaton was an androgynous being descended from Outer Space. Another, more down-to-earth report states that he was the last child descended from the marriage of a common woman who became Queen Tiy and her husband Amenhotep III.

Ikhnaton, originally Amenhotep IV, a member of a dynasty that worshiped Amon, changed his name from Amenhotep (Amon-is-satisfied) to Ikhnaton (He-serves-Aton), to reflect his dedication to Aton. He and his beautiful queen Nefertiti had six daughters—their mutual affection was openly displayed; his obvious compassion and tenderness and the portrayal of female participation in public life is evidence of a strong feminism.

Ikhnaton was mostly likely a troubled teenager, eager to get out of Thebes and out from under the priests of Amon to do his own thing, to found his City of the Horizon at what is now called Tell-el-Amarna, dedicated to the one god. He may have received his ideas about Aton from certain Mitanni women during his youth at the royal court in Thebes. The Mitannis had been ruled by Aryans. The captive women brought the deity Surya to the Egyptian court, a Vedic version of the solar god in whom the supreme power exists. Surya was initially represented abstractly as a disk, wheel, or swastika, but eventually took an anthropomorphic form.

Jeremiah certainly would have sympathized with Ikhnaton's one and only, universal god. Ikhnaton proclaimed," O thou sole God, whose powers no other possesseth, Thou didst create the earth according to Thy desire, whilst Thou wast alone: men, all cattle large and small, all that are upon the earth, that go about upon their feet; all that are on high, that fly with their wings. The countries of Syria and Nubia, the land of Egypt; Thou settest every man in his place, Thou suppliest their necessities. Every one had his possessions, and his days are reckoned. Their tongues are divers in speech, their forms likewise and their skins, for Thou, divider, hast divided the peoples."

Of course Ikhnaton did not invent worship of the Sun. In fact, he forbade the perennial worship of the Sun per se, in favor of "Heat-in-the-Sun" and Light. Naturally the perceived forms of energy should be regarded as manifestations of the Original Cause. The discoveries and inventions of our modern solar physicists would no doubt provide Ikhnaton with further verification of the wonders of Aton.

The Egyptian pantheon of gods embodied certain sacred conceptions denoted by sundry terms. Many conceptions naturally overlapped, and different terms eventually designated the same ideas. Through the hierarchical process of generalizing ultimate values, and through the competition of "my god is better than your god," certain divinities come to predominate over others in a crude pyramidal scheme, with the first family or royal trinity at its apex – in the name of the Father, the Mother, and the Son, Amen. For instance, the Sun god Re was amalgamated with the invisible god of air Amon, who was portrayed as a man painted blue to connote invisibility. The combined Amon-Re was the predominant national god who, at one time or another, could be separately considered as Amon, the prevailing god at Thebes, and Re, prevailing god at Heliopolis. Among the Hebrews, Amon was a competitor to Yahweh. The Greeks compared Amon to their Zeus—Egypt periodically sent ambassadors of Amon to Athens.

An early trinity comprised Amon-Re the Father, husband of his mother; Mut the Mother, Queen of Darkness (the Black Virgin); and Khons the Child. A later triune, stripped of the feminine element, was Re the Father; Ptah the Son; Amon the Spirit.

An Amonite hymn of the Nineteenth Dynasty states: "Amon, who came into being at the beginning, so that the mysterious nature is unknown...His image is not displayed in writing...Hidden (*amen*) is his name as Amon, he is Re in the face and his body is Ptah."

There were many other gods; one or the other god might seem to prevail here and there according to the predilection of the worshiper and the occasion—it was a common practice to flatter the god presently worshiped by saying he or she was "the sole god besides whom there is no other." Ikhnaton brought the syncretic evolution of the pantheon to focus on a single symbol of the signified divine being: Aton, the Sun-disk, symbol of divine energy radiating rays with hands at the end of them reaching out to all. The "stimulating" form of the Vedic deity Surya he was acquainted with in his youth also reached out with "golden arms" to all beings.

Aton was not concealed in an ark or in a darkened chamber at the end of a temple, nor was he the subject of occult incantations or books of the dead and weird rituals, nor was he further obscured by theological rigmarole. Quite to the contrary: Aton, although his essence was invisible, was celebrated in plain view, in the broad light of day. After all, it is impossible for any human being—except perhaps Moses, and then only by divine command—to cover up the Sun for everyone at the same time. Aton's temples had no roofs; their doors were flung wide open; there were no sacred icons or holy images within—artistic decor consisted of natural scenes, flowers, plants and animals. There was no absurd mumbo-jumbo to explain anything: Atonism simply described Aton's effulgent beauty as it is experienced in nature. There was no wrath, jealousy, revenge, thou-shalt-nots, or the static stiffness of eternity. The accent was on the positive: there was love and the lively, flowing here-and-now, and death was unmentioned; the only "shalt" was to have positive gratitude for life. The hidden was replaced by the unhidden, privacy by publicity. Aton's food was *ma'at*, or truth, which also referred to the candor of the sun and of the pharaoh's own life as it was expressed in the revolutionary "naturalism" of the contemporary art.

Ikhnaton ordered all references to Amon and plural references to "gods" hacked out with hatchets, hammers and chisels. The Egyptians were well-aware of the magical hold names have on the mind, of the pervasive influence of words inscribed on tablets and temples, tombs and other monuments; they believed the visible sign signified an invisible double that would be obliterated with the destruction of the sign; they were firm believers in iconoclasm as the antidote for undesirable gods.

While Moses' invisible YHWH was absolutely brilliant when asked for a name, responding with "I AM WHO I AM", Ikhnaton's solar disk was simply a brilliant visible symbol for one universal deity—the solar sign might be effaced, but the all powerful Sun would defiantly remain as evidence of the invisible essence of the one god. An iconoclastic nihilist could hurl dung at the Sun all day with no visible effect; of course, the Moon can eclipse the Sun, as a woman can occlude the man-child in her ark.

The only permissible personification of Aton in the City of the Horizon was the pharaoh Ikhnaton, the Son-of-Re the Father, a form of Aton. Ikhnaton was in effect the Son of God. He asserted the Divine Right of Pharaoh, an iconoclastic assertion destructive of the organized polytheistic religion of Egypt together with its political and economic trappings that had had such an enormous influence over the Empire. Many people of the old order lost their jobs and influence while newcomers found theirs.

Atonism was an abstract religion, a religion of intellectuals. Ordinary people preferred to have their vulgar icons and idols at home, and the former elite wanted their power back along with the idolization industry, wherefore the Egyptian Reformation naturally began and ended with the Rebel Pharaoh. After Ikhnaton died, Amon was easily restored along with his human sycophants. After all, the old god Amon was the triumphant god of war who had built up the Empire, while Aton the new god of Love had by virtue of his pacifism in the space of a few years lost all of it except a little corner of Palestine.

Ikhnaton ignored the desperate pleas for military help coming in from his vassals. The Empire was his personal property: he reportedly turned his cheek and gave away his cloak. His pragmatic mother Queen Tiy came down from Thebes to set him straight. A co-regent was named and sent backsliding to Thebes and its pantheon of deities. Ikhnaton's wife, Queen Nefertiti, was no backslider: she continued to adore Aton and her husband after she was sent away to a northern suburb of the dream city.

We do not know how Ikhnaton met his end. His glorious City of the Horizon was soon abandoned a few years later. General Horemheb, the commander of his army, ascended to the throne, determined to curb anarchy. He ordered workmen to destroy the signs of Aton and Ikhnaton And then Ramses the Great continued to blot out the official city of Ikhnaton, using its monuments as a quarry for the building of

Hermopolis. It became a crime to even mention Ikhnaton's name—he could only be officially referred to as "that criminal."

The Ikhnaton of popular legend was too preoccupied with ideas and ideals to ensure their protection by force of arms. The world was not ready for Love—modern writers still criticize Atonism, saying that it was an "Oriental" religion relying on the "oceanic feeling of oneness"; that is to say, Love. There is a difference between the propositions "God is love" and "Love is God." Hope remains that "God is Love" will someday express an equality relation between God and Love, so that the terms may actually be commutative. As Jeremiah reiterated so well, change has to be inscribed in hearts instead of on tablets: change has to come from a change of heart and not from an objective representation of a god. Pending that change, war shall prevail, and the will of God—whether under Name or No-name—shall try the consciences of warriors until they come into peace and harmony, wheresoever that might be.

Despite our changing archaeological interpretations, all idols, including great cities, are bound to fall.

The Goddess of Speech

I was pleasantly surprised by the vigorous responses to my little essay entitled 'Grammar,' my offering, both rebellious and humble, in my mother tongue, to Divine Mother, Goddess of Speech. Those responses encouraged me to write 'Footnote on Grammar', 'Mister Demon Raptor', 'Against Constructive Criticism', and 'Presenting Bbocchino'. I am presently further motivated to elaborate on the Mother of Language, for there is no end to Her power to generate the streams of discourse that nourish our world.

First of all, I was a little astonished by the skeptical and hostile reaction to 'Grammar, for I believed my subject was too obvious to be doubted or to be left unappreciated, and that nobody would object to my casting the subject in my own peculiar manner as an independent work of art, however dependent its success might be on somebody else's view of my grammar. The article was, in a word, an 'acroama'. That is, I intended therein to make rhetorical declamations rather than pointed arguments.

But it seems that only pointed critical arguments are acceptable to many people in this kali yuga. Hence that which that which I thought was obvious and clearly presented in my own fashion was instead thought to be vague, obscure, and mysterious to some of my audience. And, furthermore, it was given that I should have no right to be vague, obscure, and mysterious, or to give that sort of impression even if I wanted to do so.

Therefore, instead of the acroama I intended, in its exoteric sense as a common rhetorical device, my work appeared to some as acroamatic in the esoteric sense, as a secret whispering about an occult subject, if not gobbledygook.

'Acroama' means to hear: the word was once employed to denote secret oral communications. Oral communications were once considered to be far superior to written ones. As a matter of fact, some Brahmin in India still distrust written versions of the Vedas, preferring the oral tradition over the written versions and interpretations. This is not simply to maintain authority because writings can be challenged, but to establish a living personal relation, both individual and social, with Reality, rather than an empty dead-letter existence.

Or, here is a more mundane example: Aristotle would deliver an acroamatic lecture to his intimates about what his presentations to the vulgar public really meant. In my case, you must rest assured that I did not believe the general public would be too vulgar to understand me. Indeed, I leave that belief to those demeaning gate-keepers who withhold truth from the public because they whisper, acroamatically, that it would "go over the stupid heads of the audience."

Notwithstanding that whispering, it seemed from the hostility 'Grammar' aroused in some critics, that I had cast a spell on them. I even received a fax charging me with corrupting the public by intentionally misspelling 'strange' as one of its old forms, 'straunge', for special effect. In his opinion, such a practice would bring the universe of discourse to its ruin. But that was just one-half the gist of my dialectic, which he admitted he did not read in full because he was busy scanning things. It seems the average attention span on the Internet is less than two minutes, that the average brain is thus about five-hundred words long for a slow reader, a subject I addressed in my article 'Short Brains'.

'Spell' is the key word here, for there is a relation between "to cast a spell" and "to spell a word", one that goes to the radical root of my

'Grammar'. I speak of the magical and religious nature of language: the magic of coercing spirits with words, and the religion of asking for divine favors in a nice way. And I speak of the one mother tongue of all tongues and its origin, Divine Mother.

Indeed, with the magical nature of language in mind, perhaps I should have called my essay 'Gramarye' (also: gramary), instead of 'Grammar'. A gramarye is an obscure book of magic spells, a black book of unintelligible language, so named for those horrid Latin grammar primers pettifogging pedants abused their pupils with, primers written by imbeciles who thought grammar was a science! However, my article was not a brain-basher of that sort. It does, however, seem that it was a wee ark of magic spells considering the controversial issues still coming ashore.

Life for man involves intensely the life of the mind. For that purpose his Divine Mother is required. In India she is often called Vac. The impersonal form is vac, which is, of course, feminine. Vac is usually translated as "speech", "Word", and sometimes as "language" although "language" does not implicate its full purport. Vac, then, is what is uttered as well as She who utters it.

I shall hereafter use the "k" and call the Goddess of Speech "Vak." Vak is the power of the Silence before the Word is spoken as the Universe, as well as the appearance of the Universe itself. Vak is one of the many names of Divine Mother, or Sakti, the fundamental Power or Energy underlying the Universe, without which her Form or consort Siva would be a lifeless corpse. Some students believe Vak is the ultimate personification of those feminine energies called "gnas" in the Vedas, also known in ancient times as the "wives of gods."

Speech has a magical creative power or maya, a term that eventually came to signify not only something that is made, the creation, but also the power of making as well as the process of making; i.e., the triune: Maker, Making, Made. Since both men and women are born of woman, it is no surprise that Vak is female, the goddess who measures out speech; she is the Ma or Matr of Man, he whose thoughts are measured out.

The origin of the life-giving power that quickens the mind into speech as well as instigates the Universe into apparent existence is certainly mysterious, even beyond description; and despite our best scientific efforts, the material world, or what is made, often deceives us as if it were some sort of grand magic trick. What is made by mother is really there as a thing; nevertheless, our perceptions of it are often illusions, and our conceptions are sometimes delusions.

Vak's Truth is presented in mantras, or words of power, in sacred verbal formulae pregnant with riddles and infinite correlations. Vak is the Cosmic Cow from whom flows the streams, rivers, lakes and oceans of milk that constitute the Universe of Discourse. Her words are called "the footsteps of the Cow", the secret and mysterious tracks to the transcendental Truth followed by the sages.

Vak's primordial, original Truth is expressed in the single syllable OM (AUM). OM sums up Brahman, the Supreme Reality, the Universe, in an emphatic YES. The sound AUM as its three morae is the Universe of Past-Present-Future. Coincidentally, the three Greek Fates, or Morae, preside over Birth-Marriage-Death.

In India, the philosophy of Grammar is based on linguistic theology, which establishes that Wisdom, the Vedas, the words thereof, are of eternal import. That is to say that the Vedas are founded on the primacy of the Word or vac, a term comparable but not quite identical to our Logos in the West.

Grammar, then, is a 'darsana', a view of Truth, an approach to Supreme Reality, and a philosophical school. Primary emphasis is placed here on the female aspect, energy or 'sakti'. This tradition has been maintained for over 5,000 years. Vak is the Word, the "Mother of the gods", the Godhead that creates and upholds the Universe. In the Beginning there was the Word as Living Force, our Mother who is at the same time Word, consciousness, breath, and vital energy. And in the Creation there is no discontinuity between the cosmos and man the microcosm.

The Universe as it is spoken emerges in divine consciousness just as language emerges in human consciousness. But what is the Word good for? It is the means to human liberation. Yes, in the East and in the West, the object of a liberal education is ultimately liberation. And Grammar, is of course, in the West, the first of the trivium and of the seven liberal arts.

So the Word is the means to return to the Source of our speech, where we shall be freed from the chains of becoming. Why is the Baby crying? What is it that we all really want in our distress? Is it not to be picked up, to be held, to be fed with Mother's milk? And, when She puts us down, she teaches us to exchange Mother's milk for Her words, the gift of Grammar. Yet we long to return to Her arms, to Reality.

We see here that liberation runs both ways, to and fro, but ultimately freedom and absolute autonomy are fundamental characteristics only of the Godhead from whence we were born. For when the Word becomes human language it is restricted or bound by human conventions, so when I urged grammarians to rebel in my 'Grammar', I urged them to throw off those chains, to cast off the restrictions of ignorance, and to return to the arms of Vak.

As I said, Vak is one of the names associated with Divine Mother. She was originally a folk divinity who gained in influence and eventually, as men became liberated, took precedence over the great god of fire Agni. She was associated with the river goddess Sarasvati, and it would be disrespectful not to say a few words about Sarasvati, for she is adored by poets and writers as the goddess of eloquence and wisdom. Here is something from the Rigveda, one of the oldest if not the oldest statements of wisdom know to man; the hymns therein provided the singer with access to the magical powers of Vak: "So may Sarasvati, the Hero's Consort, brisk with rare life, the lightning's Child, inspire us, and, with the Dames (Gnas) accordant, give the singer a refuse unassailable and flawless." (VI 49.7, Griffith) Sarasvati ("watery, elegant") was once a famous river, now almost dried up, described as "Best mother, best of rivers" who became "best of goddesses", the tutelary deity of authors. She is presently worshiped in libraries with offerings of flowers, fruits, and incense. In ancient times, one of the most important centers of brahmanic culture was on the banks of the Sarasvati. It was said that without her water and fish, the brahmin would be too hungry to remember the sacred scriptures. She was referred to as "queen of the gods", "the melodious cow who milked forth sustenance and water", "the mother of the Vedas", "the wife of Indra, who contains within herself all worlds," and "mother of mantras." Sarasvati's most popular attributes are wealth, fatness, fertility, and ability to purify.

I hope the foregoing has served to adumbrate the goddess of eloquence to some small extent, so that others of greater vision may pierce the veil of Maya for a more illuminating view. Thus I lay my own shadow at her feet, and close with a few quotes from Madala Ten of the RigVeda. The speaker here is Vagambhrini, now known as Vak, who is describing her powers and functions:

"I go with the Rudras, with the Vasus, I go with the Adityas and the All-gods. I bear both Mitra and Varuna, Indra and Agni, and both the Asvins.

"I bear fermenting Soma, I bear Tvashtar, and also Pushan and Bhaga. I assign wealth for the sacrificer, for him that offers firsts, that presses the Soma.

"I am the queen, the assembler of treasures, the wise, the first of the worshipful ones. In manifold placed did the Gods divide me, who dwell in many abodes, causing me to penetrate many regions.

"Through me he eats food who perceives, who breaths, who hears what is spoken. Unknowing they repose upon me. Hear, O illustrious one, that which is worthy of belief I say to thee.

"I even of myself say this, an utterance acceptable to Gods and men: whomever I desire, him do I make strong, him do I make the priest, the seer, the sage.

"For Rudra I stretch the bow, that the arrow may smite the hater of the spell. For the people I make strife. I penetrate heaven and earth.

"I give birth to the father in his head. My birthplace is within the waters, the ocean. Thence I spread through all beings, and touch with my head this heaven.

"I blow forth even as the wind, reaching all beings, beyond heaven, beyond ths earth. Such have I become through my greatness."

AUM

VEDIC HYMNS, translated from the Rigveda by Edward J. Thomas, M.A., D.Litt. London: John Murray, 1923, Chapter XL. To VACH, SPEECH HYMNS OF THE RIGVEDA, Transl. H.R. Griffith, Benares: Lazarus, 1920

Faith, Belief, and Knowledge

"For we must not build temples according to the same rules to all gods alike, since the performance of the sacred rites varies with the various gods." Vitruvius

The communication or confession of faith can be beneficial to everyone concerned, yet people whose faith is perfect do not beg askance of their faith nor do they feel a need to press their faith on others, as insecure people in want of the safety of numbers are wont to do. We of lesser faith might wonder at the confidence of people who happen to have the quiet courage of their convictions, and therefore we might ask of them: What is faith? We discover from their various responses that faith may be the belief in the reality or existence of something that does not immediately appear to the senses, or the belief in the value, truth, meaning, or trustworthiness of an idea, thing, or person. And what is belief? We believe that belief accrues to the perfection of knowledge: the more we know about something, the more do we believe it. But belief is usually defined as faith in the reality or existence of something, and so on, so that in the ordinary sense of the term we have a circular definition: Faith is belief and belief is faith. Yet the terms were not always synonymous; according to the lexicographers of the *Oxford Unabridged English Dictionary:*

Belief was the earlier word for what is most commonly called *faith.* The latter originally meant, in English as well as in Old French, 'loyalty to a person to whom one is bound by promise or duty, or so to one's promise or duty itself,' as in 'to keep faith; to break faith,' and likewise in the derivatives, *faithful, faithless,* in which there is no reference to 'belief'; i.e. 'faith' was synonymous with fidelity, fealty. Since the word *faith* in Old French, *faith* or *fei,* the etymological representative of the Latin, *fides*, it began in the 14th century to be used to translate the Latin term, and in course of time almost superseded 'belief,' especially in theological language, leaving 'belief' to mean the merely intellectual process or states of the dictionary's second definition, thus 'belief in God' no longer means as much as 'faith in God.' So one might believe in God existence but not be absolutely loyalty to the Supreme Father Figure.

Now the Oxford gives the second or modern sense of faith, i.e. belief, as: "Mental acceptance of a proposition, statement, or fact, as true, on the ground of authority or evidence; or to the assent of the mind to a statement, or to the truth of a fact beyond observation, on the testimony of another, or to a fact or truth on the evidence of consciousness."

We further notice that the state of being of lief, or *belief*, is rooted in Teutonic terms such as galaubin, "to believe, probably to hold estimable, pleasing, or satisfactory; to be satisfied with." Furthermore, the Aryan *lubh*is "to hold dear, to like, whence also LOVE, LIKE." We find Caxton faithfully quoted from the year 1481, for example: "Ther ben many thynges in the world whiche ben byleued though they were neuer seen"; and Swift is quoted from 1708: "Whoever professes himself a member of the Church of England ought to believe a God." And we learn that *believe* is a misspelling of the historical form, *beleeve.*

So what was believed was that which was beloved regardless of facts, and the term faith implied what one ought to do, to believe in a powerful or superior authority whom one might not love but to whom one made a pledge or promise of faith and thereby incurred an obligation or duty.

The poet Ovid (43 B.C.E. – 18 C.E.) is translated into English as saying, "We are slow to believe that which if believed would hurt our feelings." And the Greek orator Demosthenes (384- 322 B.C.E.): "Nothing is so easy as to deceive one's self; for what we wish, that we readily believe." The great English poet John Milton (1608-1674) penned this rebellious observation: "A man may be a heretic in the truth; and if he believes things, only on the authority of another without other reason, then, though his belief be true, yet the very truth he holds be heresy." Finally, the American educator Noah Porter (1811-1892) indited: "Remember that what you believe will depend very much upon what you are." We might add that you may become something other than what you presently are by loving or believing in another state of being and therefore coming to know it according to your capacity, for knowledge is in "truth" the unity of the knowing subject and object known, a unity or identity impossible without correspondents, a relationship that is, in a word, love. For instance, as far as Narcissus is concerned, you may become the reflected god you believe in or project although there is necessarily a fatal difference in the identification, thou art that, in which both will necessary perish.

But far more interesting are the statements of faith that were made once the Latinate term *faith* was perverted – from the meaning of necessary duty towards the lords of the land to whom one swore fealty, to the cause of belief in things unseen yet beloved, especially in accord with faith in a personal form of deity set forth by religion: French emperor Napoleon Bonaparte (1769-1821) declared, "All the scholastic scaffolding falls, as a ruined edifice, before one single word – faith." Edward Young (1683-1765), the English poet, sacrificed understanding at Faith's altar, promising his fealty to the unseen Lord: "Faith is not only a means of obeying, but a principle act of obedience; not only an altar on which to sacrifice, but a sacrifice itself, and perhaps of all, the greatest. It is a submission of our understanding; an oblation of our idolized reason to God which he requires so indispensably, that our whole will and affections, though seemingly a larger sacrifice, will not, without it, be received at his hands." And we have this confusion of faith and belief from the English divine, Richard Cecil (1748-1777): "Faith makes all evil good to us, and all good better; unbelief makes all good evil, and all evil worse." Better yet, or even worse if you prefer, the English poet Thomas Russell (1762-1788) rendered faith thus: "The errors of faith are better than the best thoughts of unbelief.

Now we do not here intend to unravel faith and belief from their presently confused synonymy in order to adhere to the original distinction of their roots; rather, we endeavor to draw our own semantic distinction between the two terms as a matter of art in accordance with what one might playfully call our faithless belief or reasonable faith.

We propose that, whereas knowledge is not a prerequisite of faith, belief is perfected by knowledge. The more evidence we have of the truth of a proposition or existence of something, the more shall we believe in it and the less shall we need rudimentary faith. But the ultimate truths of religious faith are derived from a secret source, which is to admit that there is no certain sensory evidence that corresponds to the truths allegedly known.

Thomas Aquinas held that "the object of knowledge is something seen, whereas the object of faith is the unseen." His faith is forced faith or willed faith, "an act of the intellect assenting to divine truth at the command of the will moved by the grace of God." But such an assent if it be not sheer nonsense would require previous knowledge of the existence of God and his intentional revelations through miracles and other supernatural modes of communication, the truth of which cannot be verified. As John Locke noted in his essay on human understanding: "Though faith be founded on the testimony of God (who cannot lie) revealing any proposition to us, yet we cannot have an assurance of the truth of its being a divine revelation greater than our own [rational] knowledge; since the strength of the certainty depends upon our knowledge that God revealed it."

If we adhere to the old meaning of "faith," religious faith would be fealty towards an imaginary or unseen lord whose alleged commands are uttered by earthly usurpers who attend to hierarchical authority. Man's original sin is in individuality, of being divided from the whole with an inborn difference that sets him in opposition to the authorities the helpless infant needs to survive, the representatives of the terrifying world whom he must love or else, in monotheistic terms the Terrorist Almighty upon whom one depends on for salvation. A high education may substitute sublime principles for the awful impersonation.

Faith is then reserved for what we do not know but what we wish for and want to believe; and we make believe and argue that our wish has come true for fear that it is not really true or might become falsified by the loss of our power. Hence faith's harshest critics believe that blind faith in the unseen is the first and last resort of fear and ignorance, and we confess that their unwanted opinion is warranted. We are confident that the Sun will rise in the morning. Strictly speaking, we do not have faith in its rising; rather, we believe it will rise because it has risen so many times before, and we are better able to fall asleep knowing that we shall regain consciousness and arise. And we become so accustomed to rising with the Sun that we might prematurely conclude that death is a sleep from which we shall also awake one day but somewhere else again, despite the fact that we have no firsthand evidence of anyone's resurrection. Thus do we have *belief* in this world, but our *faith* rests in the next.

Certain primitive folk grew so confident in the continuation of daily life that a natural death seemed to be an unnatural event to them: It was imagined that the person who died naturally must surely have been killed out of vengeance by the ghost or spirit of someone murdered by him or somehow gravely offended by a member of his kin, tribe or clan. Eventually a god of death was blamed for taking vengeance on all humankind for the original sin of not believing in god, hence in that god their faith was placed and clung to regardless of the mounting evidence against the existence of such a god, evidence that led others not to believe in such a god at all.

Imagine that you are minding your own business during your lunch break, enjoying a strawberry-flavored sucker for dessert on Main and Walnut in downtown Kansas City, Missouri, while basking in the Sun, when a bible-thumping evangelist accosts you, leers in your face and asks, "Son, do you *balee,eeve* in God?" You are rightfully annoyed. You pull your sucker from your mouth and ask him what in Sam Hell he means by "God," and he is convinced by your question that you are avoiding his god, and that you need to be converted to his faith in order to be saved from your avoidance so that he and his flock might be further secured by an even greater number of suckers, so to speak. He tells you that you should be contemplating your death instead of sucking on your sucker, imagining how you shall burn forever in hell for your sins unless you have faith in Jesus Christ our Lord and Savior, who loved you so much that he committed suicide-by-tyrant for your sins instead of running the bloody tyrant through with a sword. The protection-racket preacher wants to put the fear of the Terrorist Almighty in you in order to convert you to the faith he professes. Apparently sucking on suckers and basking in the Sun sucks in his opinion, and is sinful to boot.

Now you may believe everything that Bible Belt preacher said until you know better, for belief is gradually perfected by knowledge unto the end of history, the fate of the individual. In fact history itself is a mistake, an elaboration of the original sin, the great mistake of necessarily imperfect, self-conscious, conditioned hence all ready doomed individual existence. In agony we may rue the day we were born. From dust to dust we go between fire and fire: The Sun gives life, but it also kills, that all vanities roasting below shall vanish in the end. How could the fire-and- brimstone evangelist go wrong when given this hell on Earth as a foretaste of what is come? But there is heaven on Earth as well, and in any case you may resent his arrogance and his insulting attitude. For all you know he is just another Elmer Gantry, a fictional conman with ulterior motives who gained his techniques from fifteen friendly Kansas City preachers who were among other queries asked by his author: 'What would you say to get people to believe in something that did not exist?'

As far as you are concerned, your faith is nobody's business but your own business, a private matter between you and your god, if you have faith in one, and you would rather keep your faith by minding your own business, for once you expose your personal beliefs someone will try to persuade you to put them down and take up their faithful version of the one-god – so it goes with the one-upmanship of the one-god within actually exalted by the preacher in all humility of his pulpit arrogance. You may believe that the doom-boosting evangelist who grovels before fate, and thinks that people must be crushed by his god to know God well, abuses his share of the blazing power overhead; you might even opine that he is the one most likely to be condemned to eternal hellfire if there is such a thing! And, if you are a Jew, a conservative rabbi might claim that you may with clean conscience hate the Christian evangelist as well, for there are two ways to kill a Jew: murder him or convert him.

What do we really know about the Unknown? We know next to nothing if not nothing at all. In fact, when we approach the insubstantial hypostasis, our definition of Supreme Being is nearly identical to our definition of absolute space. God, to use the pagan term, is nothing at all yet somehow the alpha and omega of the all. But we would not equate our nothing with ineffable nothingness, for we dread nothingness even more than we regret ourselves in particular for the defects of the particularity we hope to overcome yet somehow oxymoronically survive in indefinite form, so we refer to nothing capitalized to allude to inchoate Nothing. The Nondenominational

Gnostic knows Nothing, and he has faith in Nothing because Nothing is perfect. Knowledge of Nothing has no object, nor does it have an objective besides the realization of Nothing; and in this knowledge, which causes Socrates to feel foolish and Plato an illiterate idiot, do the wise feel absolutely ignorant. We may seem mad for saying so, but if we climb to the summit of metaphysics, we shall be made whole and see from the unity of our supreme perspective that the world is a cracked pot: All the world is mad in each and every shard; only mystics who have faith in Nothing are sane, for only Nothing is whole.

The reader might laugh at Nothing, but as Solomon said, laughter itself is proof of madness, so please suffer the foregoing foolish digression from drawing an etymological difference between faith and belief, a task to which we now return. Whosoever would fain speak etymologically in common intercourse would be misunderstood, and would therefore be perceived as a fool, or otherwise as a wise man with too much time on his hands. But who is not a fool in one way or another? Wherefore we persist in our hair-splitting endeavor, but with the caveat that we must not mistake the part for the whole, as heretics are wont to do.

To recapitulate: We have said that 'faith' originally stood for loyalty; people of good faith feared the lord, hoped for the best, and for that reason pledged themselves to his cause for safety's sake. They still voluntarily loved or 'believed' in what they really wanted for themselves. Eventually, the terms 'faith' and 'belief' became synonymous – perhaps because the lord's subjects, as they were emancipated, increasingly identified with the will of the lord as they became their own lords. Today we have distinguished faith from belief again, to say that faith is blind – perhaps because the lord, who is blind to persons as persons, would not emancipate subjects for their deeds, demanding their faith or loyalty in any event – while belief, although still signifying an object of affection, appertains to something that is known, hence is perfected by knowledge. A man may have faith in a woman, that she shall love him one day although she shuns him now. He will believe in her love to the extent he knows or is familiar with her; the foundation of such knowledge is biological or carnal, and the emotional love grows from a certain freedom of choice of mates; thus knowledge of moral and ethical principles were expressed as a wedding; for instance, Israel is the Lord's bride, the Church is the bride of Christ, and so.

In fine, we say that faith appertains to fear and hope; belief to desire and love; and knowledge to the conscious correspondence of subject and object. The better we know our subject, the better we love it, or him or her. It is said that to know god is to love god. If one's god be anthropomorphic, then to love him or her is to love one's formal self, but no form is adequate to perfection. One would be at one with one's perfect self, and we look without for examples; but

we can only find misrepresentations in others, so to avoid melancholy we fly from one thing to the next, or away from all things into the Nothing. Of that self we all remain relatively ignorant; our modern dog psychology, pig philosophy, and technology give us small consolation, for we are neither dogs nor pigs nor machines. But as self-conscious beings we do have in our madness the consolation of faith and belief in knowledge.

The Goddess Trivia

Shall we meet at the Trivium?

The origin of the word 'trivia' is no trivial matter. Indeed, the roots of words are never inconsequential. They are so important, in fact, that the old Hebrew dictionaries listed words in their root order. We might claim that since a root has its consequences in so many words, it is commonplace. But that proves its significance, not its insignificance. Moreover, an ordinary term may prove to be of uncommon import when thoroughly examined. We seldom conduct such an examination, for employing words in their etymological sense during the usual course of communications would delay and confuse discourse rather than clarify our meanings. Still, it serves our present purpose to pause and consider the original meaning of 'trivia.'

Trivia meant "three ways." In Latin, 'trivialis' appertained to the crossroads where three roads met, which came to be known, in towns, as the 'trivium', or public place. The term 'trivium' was eventually used to denote the first three of the seven liberal arts – grammar, rhetoric, dialectics – because in ancient cities teachers who could not afford to rent space rendered their services at the public crossroads, the trivium.

The earliest intersections were three-way roads, a main road eventually joined by a side road. Honest travelers encountered one another at the crossroads, yet robbers and murderers lurked nearby. Thugs entered the main roads from side paths to mug and murder their prey and run off with the plunder, leaving the victims for dead. Although evil may be found alongside good everywhere, crossroads acquired a particularly bad reputation associated with death, demons, devils, witches and company. Fortunately, certain steps may be taken in various countries to dispose of evil at the crossroads, or at least to pass it along to someone else. Sir George Frazer mentioned several proven methods in his The Golden Bough:

In England, demons may be trapped in a small log and placed at the crossroads, where passersby may contemptuously step over it to keep the devil down. It is advisable to set out food at crossroads out side of towns in Bali, and then go back to town and make a lot of noise to drive the devils out to the feast. A Chinese sorcerer may set a trap baited with wine, liver, and other goodies to catch the devils at crossroads. In Japan, rub coins on the unlucky body to transfer ill-luck to the coins; throw them away at the crossroads.

Disease may be hammered into the ground at Roman crossroads with a nail. The next passerby will catch the disease when stepping over the nail and carry it away with him. Disease may be more easily transferred to an effigy in Africa and buried at the crossroad so someone else will catch it and carry it far away. However, to do so constitutes a capital crime, subject to the death penalty. Also in Africa and elsewhere, it is best to burn the bodies of suicides at crossroads. Plato recommended in his Laws that Greek parricides be cast naked onto the crossroads; thereafter the magistrates should assemble and cast stones at the body to purify the city of criminal pollution. While in Asia be sure to drive scapegoats including human beings to the crossroads to get rid of evil. By the way, a goat may be sacrificed at the crossroads in Greece to induce the wolves to spare the flocks and herds nearby.

In Sweden, at the Midnight Fires celebration, bonfires are lit at the crossroads to scare away witches. The youth of Bohemia assemble at the crossroads on Walpurgis Night, where they crack whips to drive away the witches. On St. George's Day, Slavs have a child collect three stones from three crossroads as part of a complicated procedure to ward off witches. Most tragically, bewitched objects were once burned at crossroads in Wales so witches could then be burned there with impunity.

Given all the fuss about crossroads, we are not surprised to learn that ancient Romans set up a crossroad's goddess to protect people from evil, providing that she was adequately propitiated. Her name was Trivia, or "she-of-three-ways." 'Trivia' was a cognomen for the Greek Hecate ("far-reaching"). Today Hecate is known in her debased or vulgar form, as the Queen of Witches. Her images, called Hecataea in Greek, were set up at crossroads in ancient times to ward off evil. Her statue had three heads: that of a dog, a horse, and a lion. The three heads typified the three phases of the moon: full, waxing, and waning. A feast was laid out at the crossroads under a full moon to placate Hecate and obtain her favors. She was offered black lambs, dogs, eggs, milk, and honey. Since she was sometimes associated with Diana (Artemis), she was also called Diana of the Crossroads.

Hecate was, in her later form, a Terrible Goddess. However, at least in my opinion, she was originally a more benign and kinder goddess of production, a goddess who, like Kali, looked rather bad after men had beaten her up for a long time. The Greek poet Hesiod (8th century B.C.) said she was originally a beneficent goddess who ruled several natural spheres. Actually, very little is known about her origins. The Greeks were confused by her: they knew she really was quite different than either Selene or Artemis they eventually associated her more with Demeter and Persephone. Scholars believe she was probably an orgiastic (of course) earth goddess, a foreigner to Greece, probably from a Phrygian or Thracian cult.

Modern scholars have written off Hecate as a minor goddess, claiming that she was of no national importance to patriarchal Greece, callously underrating her as an "evil thing," a product of the decline of Hellenism. Feminists today are wont to claim that Greece was much more of a man's world than it is today. That is to say, women were property, virtual slaves to be confined indoors and to be disposed of at will. What we know of history does not support this extreme view; or at least there were exceptional women who graced the public with their virtues although jealous men figured those virtues were vices. No doubt the stronger sex held the bulk of the religious as well as the political power where religion was the worship of power, and politics was the relative distribution of that power. Although there were priestesses within some cults, women had a subordinate position in formal religion, which men allegedly fashioned with cool reason rather than fiery emotion. Women had recourse to witchcraft, to the occult, and to "hysteria" if they could get away with it. Their influence within the home was large, however, and that influence eventually grew outside of the home into a widespread mysticism which was disastrous to the old religion.

Hecate, in any event, was popular among Greek women, who were not writing many books in those days for modern philologists to unearth. Hecate was the favorite goddess of the housewife. Little images of Hecate were placed in front of doors in Athens to avert evil. She was the Mistress of Spirits to the ordinary housewife, who purified her house by smoking it and sweeping it, then taking those sweepings, along with the household ghosts therein, to the crossroads. Yes, to the crossroads, because women are tidy, and that is where ghosts belong.

Hecate was an important goddess as far as Zeus, the king of gods, was concerned. Zeus allowed Hecate the Titan to keep her three-fold powers over Earth, Sea, and Sky. In fact Hecate was the only Titan who retained her privilege. Zeus also gave her a share of Olympus. Hecate's surname was often given as Chthonia; her chthonic functions were a matter of great pride to her although she was not confined to Earth

According to an old Thessalian tale, Hecate was abandoned at a crossroads just after she was born, and was rescued and raised by shepherds. She picked up her affection for dogs from the shepherds: she is always attended by her hounds, now known as the hounds of hell. Dogs guard us from evil and have an uncanny ability to find things such as food, bodies, drugs and so on. Hecate used her dogs to hunt when not attending her flocks, so it is no wonder she was confused with Artemis. Like many women of her day, she sometimes occupied herself with a truck garden, hence she was associated with growth from decay, with the Underworld.

In the good old days, Hecate helped men obtain victory, wealth, and wisdom. She sat by kings when they judged. She brought good luck to fishermen and hunters. She worked with Hermes to increase livestock. She was the foster-mother of children. Medea, the famous Colchian sorceress who married Jason, leader of the Argonauts, was Hecate's daughter, priestess, and in effect her double. Medea was well versed in black and white magic. After she fell in love with Jason, she lulled the dragon to sleep so Jason could steal the Golden Fleece, and then went along with him on his journey, helping him with his great exploits.

But behold Hecate when male imagination runs wild during the battle of the sexes because the weaker sex deserves vengeance. What a ghastly picture she cuts. She comes our way like a bat out of hell, tall as a football field, and riding on a dragon! She is snake-footed, snake-haired, and snake-shouldered. She carries a blazing torch in one hand and a sword in the other, or, when it is extremely dark, a torch in both hands. Beware, for she carries a whip and a cord with her as well, and her hounds are howling for red meat.

Before our trivial account draws to a close, we pay due homage to Hermes, the King of the Road whom Hecate was wont to assist from time to time. Quadrangular images of Hermes were set alongside country roads and along the streets of Athens. At the crossroads, heaps of stones dedicated to Hermes were piled up as purification tallies: passersby who added stones to the piles rid themselves of guilt, especially blood-guilt due to killing. Eventually there were so many heaps of stones that they became "trivial as signposts."

Now we know that the word trivia is really no trivial matter. The term is derived from the Latin goddess Trivia, who is the Greek goddess Hecate, and whose influence is still as "far reaching" as Apollo's. If you say trivia is not trivial, and someone asks you what you mean by that, have them meet you at the crossroads where the trivium is taught.

My Notes on Thanatos

Death and Sleep are twins born of Night, and their brothers and sisters are Dreams. This morning I gradually emerged from virtual nothingness and dreamed an impersonal and wordless musing on non-existence accompanied by an senseless feeling of voidness. To which, for want of a better word, I soon applied the term "death." I feared not in this valley of death dreamed, for my royal I-ness was not in the saddle riding herd. However, when my self-consciousness was restored, my fearless feeling of lack demanded an explanation. Indeed, I felt compelled to respond to my dream at length, wherefore I began to wonder, Why did I have that vacant dream? I supposed my body was talking about its death, an inevitable event I usually heartily disapprove of although it seems to be creeping up on me nevertheless. As if death had a will of its own. As if death were a person named Death. But that is ridiculous, I insisted, for I am far from superstitious about mythological personages. Then, as I arose from my bed, the word "instinct" came to mind. Perchance the death instinct was beneath my muted dream, somewhere under my bed of existence, I opined. Why, yes, I have heard of the death instinct before, famed authors have deliberately employed it with tragic effect; but I know awfully little about it: technique is not something the creative artist wants his audience to see. Therefore I shall look into the matter from time to time. Hereunder shall appear my notes, interposed and augmented from time to time. They may or may not support an essay of two on the subject whether or not there is any such thing at all.

How does one describe or define something that may not exist or something that may not be perceived or conceived even if it does exist? I have perceived images of fantastic animals such as the jayhawk and the snark and images of mythological beings such as the gods, the grim reaper, and other monsters which are "merely" imaginary. Although such monsters are not representations of "real" beings, they are really fantastic and they do have real meanings as far as many people are concerned. Such imagery might be taken seriously by religious people, for example, for educational and inspirational purposes. But only superstitious people believe god is really in the plastic Jesus on the dashboard and therefore every drive they take under the plastic spell is divine. Nevertheless, intellectually inclined people had better not laugh too hard at vulgar idolatry for intellectuals have their idols too, albeit more sublime, in the unseen form of abstract general ideas. Indeed, intellectuals seem to be awfully superstitious about the power of ideas even when talking about them gets nothing done except perhaps the provision of slightly more gas than usual to plants. Pure intellectuals, I mean those who babble on top of ivory towers, are the most idolatrous of all people. Of course they are not recognized as such from below because they exalt invisible idols. Please have mercy on them for they seldom kill for their baubles, and every once in awhile their celestial calculations work to the practical advantage of terrestrial beings. Besides, the lions like them.

Where was I? I almost ran out of oxygen. Oh, yes, the death instinct. Now I am moved by my dream to discover the meaning of the death instinct, and I am not foolish enough to believe I can look up Death Instinct in the telephone book and give him a call. Still,I have vague notions and feelings about the meaning of death and the meaning of instinct. The combination of the two certainly seems incongruous, monstrous, and absurd to me. Evil is death and Good is life, correct? And evil is simply a negative, an absence of good, right? No doubt once that is made perfectly clear to me, ridding me of fatal error, I shall live forever. Therefore I am on the right track now that I am moved to understand the death instinct, for if evil has no positive being I shall discover my error and live forever.

Well, then, I wonder, Why don't I simply take a flying leap to faith right now and save myself the effort of beating around the bushes for the death instinct? Because I think the Persians may have been right to posit the existence of two positive gods, one evil and the other good. That *Dynamic Duo* did exist, at least in the Persian imagination, until the heretics managed to recombine them in India, eliminating evil and everywhere setting the outlaws free to be the mere absence of good again. But excuse my bush-beating. I believe my prevarications have flushed out an old image of the death instinct. I remember his name now: Thanatos!

Thanatos, bewinged and bearded personification of death, has been juxtaposed in the modern mind with Eros, the personification of love. The two gods are said to be contraries engaged in mortal combat on Earth.

In abstract terms, Eros represents the instinctive forces of organic life perpetuated in order, while Thanatos represents the so-called death instinct, a tendency to return to inorganic disorder and, ultimately, to formless chaos or Nothing. To comprehend this process, humans made a person of death and projected upon him humanity's own destructive characteristics, and made of human love another person with creative aspects.

Now the choice of Thanatos as our scapegoat may be convenient, but when we look more closely into the matter we must conclude that our version of Thanatos is an insult to the ancient Greek conception of the god. Thanatos was quite shadowy in the early days; he dressed in a black robe and carried a sword to cut a forelock from the head of the dying in preparation for the journey to the tomb or to Tartarus. In later times he was viewed as a beautiful young man who carried a lowered torch in one hand to guide the dead to their proper abode. He was usually seen traveling with his twin brother, Hypnos, or Sleep - both are gods of bodily or physical states in formal contradistinction to mental or spiritual states.

Thanatos was not shown engaged in a titanic battle with Eros. Thanatos was not on the ultimate level of conflict between being and non-being. Absolute death might be described as an absolute state of rest, or, as far as the dead are concerned, nothingness. We do not experience absolute death; to paraphrase Epicurus, we do not directly know death when we are alive, and when we are dead we know nothing about it. Epicurus did point out that it is the idea of death and not death itself which is feared by humans; his solution is to live in the moment, for a moment of pleasure in an infinite life is no more than a moment of pleasure in a finite life, hence the desire for immortality is vain.

Yet this again avoids the problem of human existence. Without complex memory and imagination there would be no humanity. Living in the now is more akin to the life of a beast than a human, and life in the moment without cognitive dampening of reticular activity can be filled with intense, immediate fear of novel objects whatever they might be. We must not ignore the meaning of death. While alive we experience partial death in grief; the body of the person we knew returns to the elements constituting it. The apparently self-moving person no longer appears, no longer has a face except for the features of his or her descendants.

Thanatos then represents the return of the bodily state to absolute rest, in contrast to the will which would have every body persist forever in perpetual motion.

Now some thinkers hold that every body, whether animate or inanimate, has an innate and essential tendency to endure to eternity. When we exercise our spiritual will in such a manner as to apply a force against a material object in order to have our way, we work to overcome its "inertia"; we consider the working force the cause of action, and the object it works upon as the passive recipient of the force exercised; however, if we reverse our perspective, we see that inertia is an opposite force, which, when equal to the force applied, brings motion to a dead stop. Therefore, apparently dead matter in the form of material objects, although they are not self-moved, seem to have an inner "life" of their own. Such objects may outlast animate beings for eons, yet they too are death bound in the universal scheme of things.

Now it might be convenient to hold ancient Thanatos to blame for what in effect is a natural process ending in Nothing or inchoate chaos, and to suppose he is locked in perpetual struggle against Eros. But in respect to his ancient Greek function, we give him far too much credit. Important as he appears to be, Thanatos plays a rather minor role in the ancient tales, as we shall soon see.

First of all, we shall review the top of the cosmic organizational chart, giving priority to Hesiod's arrangement. In the Beginning there was Chaos—infinite space. Then appeared Gaea, our "broad-bosomed Mother Earth" surrounded by the great river Oceanus. Underneath Gaea by nine-day's fall of an anvil, we have Tartarus surrounded by bronze wall reinforced with three circles of darkest night. Tartarus comprises the entire lower world, not only the hell where bad souls are punished, but the realm where good souls abide after they leave Gaea. And next on this highest level we have Eros; he is not the flighty Cupid we are most familiar with, but is the irresistible uniting force who brings order to Chaos, harmony to conflict, ruling both gods and men for their ultimate common good.

In fine, these four great gods are at the head of our organizational chart: Chaos, Gaea, Tartarus, and, last but not least, Eros. Chaos, procreating alone, begat Night and Erebus - Erebus is the personification of the three rings of darkness encircling Tartarus. Night and Erebus begat Light (Aether) and Day (Hemera), and also the repulsive ferryman, Charon, to whom the dead had to pay fare to cross over the river Styx into Tartarus.

Night, procreating alone, begat Strife (Eris). Then Strife, also alone, begat Toil (Ponos), Lethe (Forgetfulness), Famine (Limos), Sorrow (Algea), Fighting (Usmine), Battle (Mache), Murder (Phonos), Manslaughter (Androctasia), Quarrel (Neicea), Lying (Pseudea), Dispute (Amphiloggea). Lawlessness (Dysnomia), Ruin (Ate), and Oath (Horcos). Besides Strife, Night alone begat Doom (Moros), Fate (Cer), Death (Thanatos), Sleep (Hypnos), Dream (Oneiros), Blame (Momus), Woe (Oizys), Revenge (Nemesis), Deceit (Apate), Friendship (Philotes), Age (Geras), and, finally, the three Fates: Clotho who spins the thread of life, Lachesis who extends it, and Atropus who cuts it with her scissors.

All and all, with the exception of Eros at the top and friendship below, we find a gloomy cast of characters on the primordial levels of existence, Thanatos does have an important positioning under Night, but we do not discover him playing a major role. The god of the dead, Hades, who ruled over Hades, a region within Tartarus, employed Thanatos as his envoy to pick up the dead; Hades usually stayed close to home, but sometimes he did the heavy work himself, in which case his name was used instead of "Thanatos."

Thus it is said Thanatos is an aspect or servant of Hades; but given Thanatos' rank in creation, I will not cavil over functions, and simply assume Thanatos is the original god of death whose visible role was to pick up the dead. In any case, although today we might refer to the great struggle of Eros and Thanatos as the battle between life and death, it appears Eros versus Chaos would be a more appropriate bill for our ultimate tragedy except Chaos is unimaginable, an impossible role for even the best actor. That being said, let us continue on our way. No, Hades was not really inclined to act on the world stage instead of his "*alter*" Thanatos.

As a matter of fact, the more serene homebodies among the Greeks found the sight of a lovely maiden or handsome young man in the light of Day, or their loving embrace at Night, much more attractive than than the portrayal of death and its inhumane causes. The ancient Greeks were not all superstitious fools given to violent entertainments. For many the realm of the dead was simply the indefinite and mild abode of their revered ancestors presided over by the appropriate god, and not a circus of hellish side-shows imitating the destructive aspect of human nature; and death itself was not necessarily sinister. Yet even in the plays Thanatos (or Hades) was usually kept out of sight; human actors representing humans and gods took care of the killings. Indeed, poets were inclined raise hell to Earth, often employing their imagination to aggravate instead of ameliorate the passions. Nevertheless, we must not think that all Greeks were so barbarous in politics and religion as we might presume from the tales of horror.

I said we want to hide death. But if we consider death as the "death instinct" as personified by Thanatos, we discover that Thanatos keeps himself hidden without much effort on our part. He is a trickster. And how does he trick us? He causes each of us believe we are exceptions to the iron-clad rule that all people die. In the heat of battle with death in full view all around, the warrior, short of panic, believes he will nevertheless survive. The longer he survives the more he believes it. He becomes fatalistic, and the sight of corpses all around begin to appear as just so much dead matter.

It is unnecessary to hide the casualty statistics from the soldiers, for enough of them believe they are exceptions to the odds against their survival, even though their entire number might be wiped out several times during the course of a war, to press on. As Freud put it: "No instinct we possess is ready for a belief in our own death." On the way to the Front in the Great War, British soldiers sang, "The bells of hell go ring-a-ling/For you but not for me." An ironic joke, yet one believed in. Since Death is a trickster, he might be tricked. Sisyphus, the king of Corinth, tricked Thanatos: when Thanatos came for him, he tied him up, thus depriving Hades of new occupants. Unfortunately, Zeus came to the rescue.

Some say Ares, the god of war, conducted the rescue operation, presumably to make war worthwhile. Some warriors who love war say that what they love is not the killing of others but rather the thrilling possibility of their own destruction; although the chances of it are, as we have mentioned before, very slim, but still...

In yet another story, Sisyphus descended into Hades to cheat death. I might trace the career of this crafty sophist elsewhere. He is presently pushing a boulder up a hill so it will roll back down again for him to push up again, and he is under the vigilant eye of the warden; therefore, like the Sun, I presume he will be available on my return for an interview in this life or the next.

Returning to Thanatos, Homer gives slight mention of him in the context of the Trojan War. We do find the rudiments of Greek religion in the Homeric tales; rather, in the Homeric sacred scripture. We are hardly surprised to find a close association between religion and death anywhere. In a sense, religion is an organized reaction to the fear of death; fear is overcome through the worship of Power, and that worship encourages the struggle for survival.

During World War I, soldiers reported they saw angels hovering over the battlefields. They saw and heard ghosts in the trenches. Once the soldiers were on the battlefield awhile, they were no longer impressed with the jingoistic religious nationalism and its political theology. But the Christian love-religion motivated many Christians soldiers to march onward in war. One widely circulated story reported the Germans had actually crucified a soldier in full view of his fellows. Such a view would certainly torment the victim's comrades, but not to flee in panic; rather, in their brotherly or platonic love, they would be moved to keep up the killing with a vengeance, perpetuating, as in a Greek play, Thanatos' chain of death. Of course Christians were well aware of the conflict of their position, that of love-inspired hatred. A trench paper called the *Murdock* put this verse in the mouth of a chaplain:

"I do not wish to hurt you But (Bang!) I feel I must. It is a Christian virtue To lay you in the dust. You - (Zip! that bullet got you) You're really better dead. I'm sorry that I shot you - Here, let me hold your head."

Homer relates how the Lycean hero, Sarpedon, a son of Zeus and an ally of the Trojans, was incensed when the Greeks slaughtered his allies wholesale one day. Enraged, he attacked the Greek hero Patroclus, and after a furious contest, Sarpedon was slain.

Zeus had wanted to prevent the death of his son, but Hera pointed out that, if he saved Sarpedon's life, then other gods would act likewise, which would in part defeat the purpose of the war. Now before Sarpedon expired he urged his kinsmen Glacus to rally the Lyceans and Trojans against the Greeks.

A terrible fight ensued, during which Patroclus gave orders that Sarpedon's bronze armor be stripped from his body as a prize of war. That the Greeks managed to do without interference and they triumphantly carried it back to their ships. However, Zeus would not permit the Greeks to mutilate Sarpedon's body. At Zeus' bidding, Apollo carried the corpse from the battlefield, clothed it in immortal garb, anointed it with ambrosia, and then handed it over to Thanatos and Hypnos; they in turn transported it not to Hades, but to Lydia, the homeland of the deceased.

Apollo comes into contact with Thanatos again in Euripedes' play, *Alcestis*, a play about an old Greek myth. When the Greeks went to such a play they already knew the full story; furthermore, they enjoyed seeing the play repeated. They knew Alcestis was the daughter of King Pelias. Her sisters were persuaded by Media to cut up their father and boil him in herbs to rejuvenate him; of course the insane remedy did not work. Alcestis was the only daughter who did not participate in the absurd effort to save the father they all loved so much they killed him. Alcestis was thereafter wooed and won by Admetus, and she bears him fine children. But alas, he discovers he will die young. He asks Apollo, who is tending Admetus' cattle, for help. Apollo visits the Fates and manages to trick out a deal whereby they will take Alcestis in exchange for Admetus. Alcestis insists on saving her husband with her death; he agrees to the substitution. As a consequence, he not only suffers grief but intense guilt and remorse, and he envies his wife her death. Hercules appears at the palace; Admetus plays the perfect host, taking in the traveler without mentioning his terrible plight. When Hercules discovers from the servants what has transpired, he is so impressed with his host's good hospitality that he resolves to wrestle Alcestis from the grasp of Thanatos; or, if need be, to descend to Hades and retrieve her. Euripedes' play proceeds with a scene outside the Thessalian palace of King Admetus. Apollo enters - I quote from Alistair Elliot's translation:

"APOLLO Halls of Admetus! Here I made myself, a god Accept the food of slaves, Because of Zeus, who killed my son Asclepius With a bolt of fire throught the heart; Angry that I killed the blacksmiths of his terrible flame, The Cyclopes; my father, in penalty, Forced me to slave under a mortal man. I came to this land, grazed the cattle for my host, Kept his house safe till now; For, loyally serving I found a loyal master, Pheres' son, Admetus. I eventually rescued him from death, Tricking the Fates; those goddesses promised me He should escape an immediate end If he paid in exchange another life to the ones below. He went trying in turn all who were dear to him And found nobody but his wife who was willing To die in his place and no longer look at light. Now she is held up in his arms there, Her soul breaking from her, because today Is fated for her death, her changing out of life. And I, for fear of catching the taint of mortality in the house Am leaving this roof, the dear halls.[*Enter* Death] - (Thanatos) "Already I see Death near. There he is, the priest of the dead, To lead her down to the house of Hades; He has come hard on time, watching the day When she must die."

Apollo makes a half-hearted attempt to persuade Thanatos to go find someone who is riper for death than Alcestis, someone older whose time is due, pr someone who lived long enough to afford a rich burial. Thanatos says,"My prize is greater when the dead are young." He accuses Apollo of favoring the rich who would be glad to buy longer lives. Thanatos claims his right to the dead when due. "You understand my ways," he says. Apollo replies, "Hateful to men, detested by gods." Thanatos: "You can't have everything that is not yours." Apollo exits; Thanatos has the last word:

"DEATH You could *say* a lot; you'd gain no more by it: The woman will go down to the halls of Hades. I am walking to her now To begin the ceremonies with the sword, For, all whose heads this sword shaves clean of hair Are holy to the gods below ground."

Thanatos is known for taking only a forelock of hair, and this reference of a cleanly shaven head reminds us of nuns who commit themselves to the hereafter. Although in this play Alcestis will be saved from Thanatos by Hercules, her salvation is only a reprieve. Myth provides Alcestis with a seat of honor next to Persephone, Queen of the Dead, and her grave on Earth is not the abode of a dead woman but a shrine to her incomparable virtue in sacrificing herself for her husband. Thus we have here an instance of the relation between Eros and Thanatos, wherein the self is destroyed for the beloved. We must also recall that her father was destroyed by his loving daughters in order to save him. And we know of parents who have murdered their families in order to save them, and so on. Yet in this case Admetus has saved only himself by sacrificing what he loves the most. He is inconsolable:

"ADMETUS What can be worse for a man Than losing his wife? I wish I had never married And shared a home with her. I envy the unmarried, the childless - They have one life, and its grief Is not too great a pain. But the illnesses of children, the wedding Beds plundered by deaths, It's unbearable to see that. If you can, Go unmarried and childless through all your life."

His words of woe run on and on, and they are not appreciated by the Chorus: "You put no limit to your pain... Endure it: you are not the first to lose a wife." Then they speak of Necessity, a goddess known as "the Strong Fate", an abstraction of the Three Fates to whom even Zeus is arguably subject since he is not their father. Now the Chorus sings to the concept of necessity:

"CHORUS ...She alone of the gods had no Altar and no image for us To approach, she listens for no sacrifice. O Goddess, do not come down Greater on my life than ever. For even Zeus fulfills his Wishes only with your help. Among the Chalybi you tame Iron with your strength; there is no Soft respect in your abrupt will. "Admetus, the goddess has taken you in her bonds, Her inescapable hands, But endure it, for you will never bring the dead Back from below by weeping. Even the sons of gods in darkness Waste away in death. She was dear when she was with us, Dear still now she is gone. The finest of all women Was the wife of your bed. "Let us not think of your wife's tomb as A mound for the mortal dead; Let honor be paid there as to the gods, A shrine of travelers. One going down in slanting path will say, 'This one died for her husband once, Is now a blessed presence here - O Lady, give us good fortune!"

Many critics have little respect for Admetus, for he brought his grief upon himself by allowing his devoted young wife die for him. But the gods work in mysterious ways. And we might ask, "Is it not supremely heroic, even godly, to accept the highest gift any human being can offer, her life?" The ancient practice of widow-sacrifice among the ancient warriors has also been heavily criticized, but we must not forget the heroism of the widows and maids who voluntarily mounted the pyres to honor husbands and nations. Good hospitality and good wives, the pride of the Greeks; and bearing grief well with the proper rites was also insisted on.

As I have mentioned above, bearing grief is about the only way we experience death, and that experience prepares the way for our own death. But still we hope to cheat Thanatos, the scapegoat for our own ills, or our ill-will called "death instinct," of his simple right to the dead.

We hope to descend like Orpheus to resurrect the dead. Many poets have sung songs about this seemingly impossible quest to cheat death. I suppose sane people have "closure," and surely "time heals" many them in the long run. But some of us are never healed, and we continue to grieve unto our own demise.

I know this from personal experience, and even more so my father: since the death of Charlotte, we would not give her up. The trails through the underworlds have been the torments of hell in contrast to our hope. But I shall not continue here in this personal vein. Suffice it to say that, if the Orpheus Complex has not been heretofore recognized, then I recognized it here and now by that name.

Hercules is now on the scene in Euripedes' play. He resolves to retrieve Alcestis - it is difficult to ascertain whether she is actually dead or just about dead during the foregoing scenes. In either case, she is saved by Hercules, who gives her hand to Admetus. She speaks not a single word in the entire play.

"HERACLES ...For I must save the lately dead Wife, Alcestis, and settle her in this house again, Paying Admetus' favor back. I will go and look out for Death, The black clothed king of the dead; I think I'll find him near the tomb Drinking the blood of sacrifices there. And if I rush from a hiding place and catch him, And throw the circle of my arms around him, Nobody shall free him, his ribs aching, 'Til he give up the woman to me. Or, if I miss my prey there And he doesn't come to the clotting blood, I will go down to the sunless house of those below, Persephone and her king, and ask for her. I trust I'll bring Alcestis back up here And put her in my host's hands. He took me in instead of driving me away, Though struck with heavy misfortune. But he hid it nobly, out of respect for me. Who is more welcoming in Thessaly? Or in Greece? No, this *noble* man shall not say He did a kindness to someone contemptible."

The Mysterious E and The Egg at Delphi

L*eto's all-glorious son goes to rocky Pytho, playing upon his hollow lyre, clad in divine, perfumed garments; and at the touch of the golden key his lyre sings sweet.* Hesiod

Zeus sent two golden eagles, one from the East, the other from the West. Their meeting located the center of the world at a place we call Delphi. Their juncture was commemorated with a stone egg, an 'omphalos.' Upon the world-egg is inscribed four letters, the last three of which spell the original name of the great Earth goddess, Gaea.

Gaea's shrine was right there, below snowy Parnassus, long before Apollo slew Python, the dragoness guarding it, and seized the real estate for his cult; a murder and grand larceny for which he served eight years at hard labor to purge his blood-guilt. Poets sometimes called Delphi, "pytho", or "I rot", for there hot Helios caused the she-dragon's flesh to rot. If we are to believe Hesiod, she deserved her demise, for "Whosoever met the dragoness, the day of doom would sweep him away."

The dragoness's sidekick was Hera's spite-child, the monstrous Typhoeus, whose successors, in the form of typhoons, still wreak havoc about the globe. A form of Typhoeus also plagues modern human society in the form of television and the World Wide Web: "Out of his shoulders came a hundred fearsome snake-heads with black tongues flickering," reported Hesiod in his *Theogony*, "and the eyes in his strange heads flashed fire under the brows; and there were voices in his fearsome heads, giving out every kind of indescribable sound." Today his myriad writhing legs, as we can see, are plugged into electric sockets.

Hera conceived this monster alone, without the help of intercourse with her unfaithful husband, because she was jealous of Athena, who was conceived and born without her aid from the head of Zeus.

Another, less popular, history of the possession of the temple's site states that Gaea conveyed part of the estate to her daughter, Themis, goddess of prophecy and law, long before Apollo got hold of it, proving that a male was not required for its lawful administration. Themis, in turn, turned over her share to Apollo. Gaea had also shared the property with Poseidon; he gave his share to Apollo in exchange for an island. Thus did Apollo gain full title to the realty.

The first letter of the four letters on the stone half-globe marking the property is a crude 'E', standing on its three legs as if it were a tripede preparing to walk—the right leg is bent forward. The E also looks like a temple with its roof overlapping on each end.

The meaning of the E has been a mystery since ancient times. Experts do not agree, wherefore we may speculate at our leisure on the meaning of E. The Greek name for the letter E is EI, a diphthong denoting the number five. The term is also the word for 'IF', as well as the word for the second person singular of the verb, 'to be', or, 'thou art.' E also stands for 'temple' in one of the Semitic languages. The Semites were of course in communication with the Greeks; EL was the name of their Sun-god or Sky-god, whose house was 'high' or in 'heaven.' Common sense may lead us to believe that the four letters mean "Thou art Gaea", or "The Temple of Gaea" or "The Egg-House of the Goddess."

We may take a numerological approach to E. Besides the E on the omphalos, there was an E inscribed somewhere on the temple itself, next to maxims such as Know Thyself, Nothing Too Much, A Pledge Causes Trouble. There may have been four other maxims, including Falsify the Coin, and E, if we count E as a maxim, and another two, unknown, for a total of seven maxims—our lucky number, seven, was

Apollo's prime number. The Seven Wise Men were said to be authors of the seven maxims. That jibes with Apollo's number seven, but not with E as the fifth letter of the alphabet. Mind you then that two of the Seven Wise Men were believed to be impostors—at least five of the seven wandering wise men allegedly impeached two of their number for plagiary while on the road. Let's take that road back to Delphi and consider the politics circumambulating the sacred E.

The Political Religion

Delphi became the vatican (prophetic) city and catholic (universal) center of the ancient Greek religion administered by the cult of Apollo, which enjoyed the imbibing of mead, fermented honey deemed an aid to the reasoning power. Dionysus horned in on the mead drinkers early on; many were those who came under the influence of his wine, which inflamed the passions. Apollo was loyal to Zeus: he did not try to replace him, but served as his administrator.

Delphi, besides being the location of Apollo's primary residence, was replete with treasury buildings or national banks, a theater and other structures. Its political protector was the Amphictyony, a league of Greek nation-states—an ancient Greek precursor of the modern League of Nations. Members of the league were not supposed to destroy each other's cities or cut off their water supplies in time of war or peace, and they agreed to make war on anyone who violated the rules. Naturally, the Amphictyony was subject to the usual bickering, back-stabbing, double-dealing and double-crossing characteristic of political leagues.

Religion worships absolute power while Politics distributes it. The religious institution at Delphi was subservient to the political factions that combined against foreigners, and occasionally warred against each other for control of the temple and its accumulated treasure. The cult's main concerns were the ritual purification of homicides of their blood-guilt, immigration law, and drafting constitutions of foreign colonies.

Its priests or monks, who, along with the Pythias or nuns, belonged to an order of Cretan religious, had considerable influence. Knowledge is power; they possessed the power of information brought to the international center: they were often consulted by foreigners.

Myth relates that the original priests were Cretan merchants sailing a black ship upon which Apollo leapt in the form of a dolphin, took control of the helm and sailed it to Crisa below the glades of Parnassus; he identified himself as the son of god, and instructed them to administer his new temple, its altar to be called Delphinius (dolphin); the merchants worried they would not make a living in the middle of nowhere; Apollo Delphinius called them fools and said that, if they kept his temple with righteousness in their hearts, they would never want for wealth no matter how much they consumed. Thereafter the priests interpreted the Pythia's hysterical ejaculations from her tripod and rendered her prophecies as poesy. The findings usually favored the faction most likely to win; yet the prophecies were conveniently ambiguous in the event something went wrong that might cast doubt on the temple, or simply to avoid suspicion of treason when the favored party was an enemy to the Greeks. Although politically oriented, the temple never had the sort of political power that the Roman Catholic Church obtained by coincidence - or, if you will, by the will of its god.

We know that the Delphic institution existed at least a thousand years before our Common Era. The religion of the dead and the cult of immortality associated with Dionysus was introduced in the eighth or ninth century B.C.E. The fifth-century B.C.E. temple at Delphi was destroyed and rebuilt in the fourth century. The rebuilt temple suffered partial destruction about 84 B.C.E. It was damaged again in Nero's time, and eventually fell into disrepair. Apparently the Romans gilded the letters of the maxims when they restored them, presumably because the Seven (or Five) Wise Men had provided the original maxims writ in gold on tablets. Plutarch, who is almost our sole source of information about the mysterious E, speculated on its meaning in his little book,

The E at Delphi, wherein he mentioned that it was "the golden E of Empress Livia." Augustus Caesar's wife may have been saddened that the temple had become so run-down by her day, and had the E on the temple itself gilded or re-gilded.

Speculations

The illustrious letter E at Delphi presented a mystery to visiting speculators in ancient times. They were not inclined to believe that its appearance was an accident. At least Plutarch thought not in *The E at Delphi*:

"For the likelihood is that it was not by chance nor, as it were, by lot that this was the only letter that came to occupy first place with the god and attained the rank of a sacred offering and something worth seeing; but it is likely that those who, in the beginning, sought after knowledge of the god either discovered some peculiar and unusual potency in it or else used it as a token with reference to some other of the matters of the highest concern, and thus adopted it."

Love does not abhor a secret, and religion loves mystery. Sometimes it is convenient to desist from efforts to solve the riddles of life, and, after a leap to faith, to refer to god's mysteries when questioned about the embarrassing contradictions between words and deeds. But metaphysicians seldom tire of playing the game of riddles; nor do they mind the proverbial futility of their philosophy, for, as one of the greatest philosophers pointed out, seemingly vain and useless endeavors give useful ones more meaning and sometimes result in practical theories of substantial benefit to humankind.

Plutarch attended a philosophical workshop held at Delphi on the meaning of E and other Delphian things. He recounted that the philosopher Ammonius (Plutarch's teacher Ammonius of Athens, a first century expert on Aristotle) said that Apollo was no less a philosopher than a god, as is evident from his titles: Inquirer, Clear, Disclosing, Knowing, Conversationalist.

"Since," quoth Ammonius, "inquiry is the beginning of philosophy, and wonder and uncertainty the beginning of inquiry, it seems only natural that the greater part of what concerns the god should be concealed in riddles, and should call for some account of the wherefore and the explanation of the cause. For example, in case of the undying fire, that pine is the only wood burned here. while laurel is used for offering incense; that two Fates have statues here, whereas three is everywhere the customary number; that no woman is allowed to approach the prophetic shrine; the matter of the tripod; and the other questions of this nature, when they are suggested to persons who are not altogether without mind and reason, act as a lure and an invitation to investigate, to read, and to talk about them."

And indeed the investigations of Delphi continue to this very day, with ample doubt in mind, not only as to the meaning of E, but, for instance, as to the role that women played at Delphi. If only we could ask a pythia or sibyl for the meaning of the E. Of course we would still have to interpret her rant.

Woman's Crucial Role

The fair sex played the leading and perhaps only role at the prehistoric site long before Apollo arrived on the scene to slay Mother Earth's dragoness, the Python. After the far-shooting god's Cretan priests or "holy ones" took over the administration of the sacred precinct, they could not do without the enthusiasm of women for long, wherefore a virtuous woman called the pythia or pythoness was recruited to eat the bay leaves or laurel; drink of the sacred spring; sit on the tripod; inhale the gas seeping from the crevices; and serve as Apollo's medium. The priests in turn would interpret her uttering for the benefit of inquirers.

A pythia was probably a trained nun of the Cretan order whose performance on the tripod was sincere play-acting. Or she might have been a free-born Delphian woman of the lower classes, relatively ignorant and superstitious, with a hysterical temperament possibly aggravated by the subterranean dream-gas seeping up through the crevices. In any case she was pure enough to receive and to convey Apollo's seminal data unadulterated. Young virgins were tried at first, but certain disturbances led to the employment of matrons over fifty, who, to maintain the appearance of propriety during the purification process, wore the attire of young maidens.

In any case, the immediate organ of divine inspiration, the balloon of divine inflatus, was always female. Furthermore, ancient sources besides Plutarch have stated that women on the whole were in fact allowed entrance the inner shrine, and that the sacred fire was attended by elderly married women. Students of the cult now believe that women were never excluded from the whole temple, and that they enjoyed the same consultative privileges as men.

Among the women about the sacred grounds of "rocky Pytho" were the sibyls, old women who sang pessimistic prophecies—their pioneering practice influenced the Jews, then the Christians. In fact the very first sibyl is believed to have set up shop by a rock just south of Pythian Apollo's temple. Pausanias wrote in his travel guide of a later sibyl who sang her prophecies by that rock, 'Sibyl Rock' or the 'Rock of Herophile.' Pausanias said that this Sibyl Herophile, in her 'Hymn to Apollo', called herself Artemis as well as Herophile; she claimed to be Apollo's sister as well as his daughter, and said her mother was a nymph of Mount Ida and her father a man.

"I was born between man and goddess, slaughterer of sea monsters and immortal nymph, mountain-begotten by a mother of Ida, and my country is sacred to my mothers, red-earthed Marpessos, the river Aidoneus."

A sibyl at Delphi foretold the troubles to be caused by Helen, reputedly the most beautiful woman in the world. Some authors believe 'the monstrous regiment of women' are at the root of war and revolution; for instance, Thomas Jefferson thuoght Marie Antoinette caused the French Revolution. Arnold Toynbee collected a list of notable femme fatales for his history. Women have of course produced more good than evil. Their mysterious motivating power over men is undeniable. Given the brutes women were given to tame, they occasionally resorted to occult methods instead of direct confrontation, say 'womb-like convulsions' and mantic or manic shrieking, to produce their tangible and intangible goods. 'Rational' men in several regions eventually subdued and monopolized the 'irrational' arts, saving the priest and killing the sorceress as per patriarchal holy scripture.

Suffice it to say that woman played the crucial spiritual role at Delphi. Even in politics, she had far greater influence than supposed by modern historians who want her tied to the bedpost. Since she laid the egg or 'Navel' found at Delphi, upon which was inscribed the mysterious E, we may consult her on the meaning of E amongst other things.

Take Five

Perhaps the meaning of the Greek E was no mystery to those who actually spoke the prosaic language at the time. As we have pointed out, the fifth letter of the alphabet signified the number five, and it also stood for 'if' and for 'thou art.' Yet its gilded presence, standing by the maxims inscribed somewhere on the temple at Delphi, provided the metaphysicians with occasion to climb above the merely mundane meanings of E into the transcendental spiritual sphere enlightened by Apollo, who himself was upwardly mobile, having once been a herculean cave man, but became a shepherd, and then emigrated over pastures to the city where he took his seat as the brilliant minister or Sun of Zeus—he still resided in the suburbs, however, in his sacred cave.

We have found a curious old coin depicting the ancient temple at Delphi. The mysterious E appears on the coin in the same form we use for our own capital 'E'. It is suspended in mid-air, between three columns on its left and three columns on its right. Perhaps this E is the key to the temple and its universe of divine intercourse. Hesiod said Pythian Apollo struck a "golden key" there on his lyre; then, as swift as thought, he sped from Earth to Olympus, to the house of Zeus, where the immortal gods were assembled to think only of the lyre and song. Upon his arrival he accompanied the sweet voices of the Muses - they hymned the infinite gifts of the undying gods and sang of the miseries mere mortals suffer at their deathless hands.

It is interesting to coincidentally note that the fifth semi-tone of the chromatic scale starting from C is E, and that E is the fifth tone in the relative minor scale, A minor. An argument has been made that the key of E Major is the musical key to the universe. Other keys have their advocates. More interesting is the fact that the most important concordant musical interval after unison and octave is the fifth, found by Pythagoras when he moved the bridge on a single string to the proportion 3:2. His tuning system was based solely on fifths. He believed that the entire universe was inherent in numbers, and heard in planetary motion the music of the spheres. Since we mentioned the ratio 3:2, we recall that five is the sum of the first even and the first odd numbers, two and three. The two of course is female and the three is male, so we have a marriage in five. Furthermore, multiples of five give us a product divisible by five or ten. The wise men of Greece counted by the great 'pempad' or by 'fives.' Ten is the perfect number; would anyone with ten fingers want one less or one more digit, or one less or one more hand? Wherefore five produces nothing but itself or perfection.

That is not the only reason five is excellent and the number ten is perfect around the world, but let us move on, for we do not have time to get our numbers straight here. After all, every number up to perfect ten has its occult qualities about which we could converse almost ad infinitum.

While at the temple of Delphi, which was blessed by one of Nero's visits, Plutarch recalled a remark he heard made by Ammonius several years prior—during a lively discussion of the meaning of the mysterious E: "It is not worthwhile to argue too precisely over these matters with the young, except to say that every one of the numbers will provide not a little for them that wish to sing its praises."

Eustrophus the Athenian, who found all principles human and divine reposed in the theory of numbers, said, "E is not unlike the other letters either in power or in form or as a spoken word." He claimed that E was held in high honor because of the custom of counting in fives.

Apologia For The Muttering About Delphi

On so-called snooty academic driveling regarding dragon sexuality, Delphi, Goddess Trivia

Introduction

I have just received a message asking me to "translate the enclosed obscure academic muttering into plain English to determine if anything has really been said or if the words are merely the snooty academic driveling of a frustrated ivory-tower humanist." Much to my embarrassment, the enclosed "muttering" was the first paragraph of my extended article on dragon sexuality, as follows:

The Muttering

"Where the three paths divide and migrate from their origin, where the decision tree first branches off in two directions no matter from what direction it is approached, ambiguity presides, there, in the streaming flux, by the cave where the dragon sleeps. At the spiritual crossroads, or Trivium, the hysterical maiden perched on the tripod gives birth to ambiguous oracles for men to contemplate and swaddle in interpretive textiles of various designs and qualities. Some weavers become so entranced by their own designs that they ignore the goddess Trivia at the mundane crossroads where thugs often lurk, and go into the uniform business there, so that entire armies might glorify their logical designs. War then becomes fashionable, and the bewitched myrmidons march without scruple under delusions of grandeur divided, forgetting that fashions are fleeting and that, in the cosmic scheme, soldiers are ephemerons, or short-lived insects in the minds of their gods. As in war, so in its political substitutes, where ideologies based on logical dichotomies reduce the ideologues to a general ignorance of truth or to, in a word: imbecility."

Statement of Intent

Herculean as the task appears, I intend to interpret the paragraph. At first glance, its meaning is perfectly clear to me. After all, I wrote it. But to say something simply and clearly can be very difficult. A ballet dancer or musician will tell us that it is no easy matter to perform the simplest choreography or song perfectly. Indeed, I have seen professional performers fall apart in slow classes because they do not have an adequate foundation: they have gotten away with rushing through things and glossing over fundamental weaknesses with fast and fancy footwork or fingerwork. Perhaps my intellectual calisthenics ran away from their foundations. Maybe there is no meat in the paragraph so rudely returned to me: that remains to be seen, so I will valiantly attempt to interpret it and resubmit it to my readers so they can judge whether it really means anything at all or is just much sizzling without any steak.

PROSAIC PURPORT OF THE MUTTERING

When men have difficulty making crucial decisions, they consort privately with women, then embark on various adventures according to their selfish interpretations of what has transpired.

DISCUSSION

Cultivation of Hysterical Women and Reasonable Men

Since time immemorial, men have enjoyed the right acquired by might of making most of the important decisions for their families, clans and nations. No doubt prehistoric women were fierce enough to put up a good fight when their lives were threatened, but men had the definite physical advantage. Control of the womb, the primary private property, went to the men who battled for it along with the rest of the ground of life.

Although the respective roles of men and women have varied and reversed over time and place, the civilization imposed by men kept women at home and in garden, and men in the political arena and in the battlefield. This gender segregation was conducive to the development of two forms of communication, or languages. It is no great leap to the eventual conclusion that men wound up speaking the public language of "reason" while women spoke the private language of emotion, or that men are more objective and women are more subjective in their affairs.

Given their intimidating circumstances, it is hardly surprising that females relied on tactical weeping, sulking (including suicide) and on throwing fits to get their message across rather than resorting to direct confrontation. These seemingly irrational and spontaneous outbursts were of course associated with the bloody secrets of birth, menstruation and other occult subjects better avoided by men, hence the feminine mystique deepened over time into a mystical sort of religion. We have here the "hysterical" (hystero: uterus) woman as opposed to the "reasonable" (ratio-calculating) man. Not that woman was a fool, not by any means: she was as wise as the serpent. Men wanted her and needed her. She was, first and foremost, their mother. As for her hysterical mystical power, later associated with romance, men worked on appropriating that for "reason" until they were able to convince themselves that enthusiasm (god-possession) is reasonable in a man, but in a woman it is mental illness: "hysteria", "uterine furor", and even "nymphomania", the teenager's favorite myth. Cultivated men would eventually get away with romantic weeping, with wearing makeup, gowns, wigs, frilly blouses and such, while retaining their reason and machismo.

The Pythia

Be that as it may, the occult powers of so-called hysterical women were respected and feared in ancient times, which brings us to "the hysterical maiden perched on the tripod (who) gives birth to ambiguous oracles for men to contemplate" mentioned in my "muttering" here discussed. I am referring to the prophetess at Delphi in ancient Greece, called the "pythia". She was so named after the female (later poets performed a sex change operation on her) dragon Python, whom Apollo slew when he seized the temple from the Earth Mother cult. The dragon was guarding the usual treasure, the Egg or Navel of the universe. The office of the pythia was established after the seizure as a sort of compensation to the old matriarchal interests. The pythia was originally supposed to be a young virgin because virgins allegedly retain their innocence and can deliver unstained messages from the glorious god. Since the oracle at Delphi, located in the center of the Greek world, symbolized the unity of the Greek states, the pythia was the untouchable national virgin. However, a Thessalian named Echecrates fell in love with her, swept her away and had his sacrilegious way. After that, it was duly decided than only a matron of fifty could fitly serve as the pythia.

Of course, the pythia was a hysterical woman when she was delivering her incoherent mutterings, which the male priests gladly translated into rather bad verse as the offerings poured into the sacred treasury. (Scholars believe the pythia was actually a member of an order of nuns originating in Crete). Roughly three thousand years later, the debate continues as to whether the "hysteria" and related prophetic "hallucination" were phenomena induced by gases and drugs. The pythia chewed laurel leaves and drank from a stream in preparation for the prophetic occasion. She may have been lowered into a chasm filled with gasses—new research (1998) has revived that possibility, long laughed at by experts who thought they were in the know because of an inadequate archaeological excavation. How stoned can one get on leaves? What was in the water? Some spiritual substance in the underground, unconscious flux might have been involved, watched over by the dragon—beware, dragons have a habit of rising up again after being slain and left to rot in pits.

The pythia sat for the séance on a "tripod" or three-legged affair of such fascinating mystical significance that I cannot delve into it here except to say it is related to the Three Paths. She rendered her mutterings in response to particular questions put to the oracle by notable men: for instance, political leaders who posed questions as to whether or not they should make war. Keep in mind here that the Delphic oracle was the international womb of the Greek states. There were several Sacred Wars to possess her. The Delphic oracle served the usual religious-political function (religion pertains to Power and politics to its distribution): that being the spiritual-intellectual justification for the regulation of man's basic urges for food, defense, and sex. Once the international virginal womb was secured by Apollo at Delphi, and the food and drink rituals established, the primary concern was the expiation of blood-guilt, the regulation of murder.

The presiding god at the oracle, Apollo, who eventually reached far and wide with his arrows, was not originally a Sun-god: he was an ex-cave man who immigrated from the wild to farm then to town, hence he was the god of immigration and colonization. His temple at Delphi was devoted to the development of Greek unity and of international law. That temple was under the guardianship of the Amphictyonic Council, an assembly of twelve northern Greek nations more infamous for meddling and trouble making than famous for keeping peace by means of their international laws regulating war.

What influence the prophecies rendered at Delphi might have had is a scholar's bone of contention. Some authorities believe the priests who interpreted the pythias' utterings were the usual priestly conservatives careful for their own skins, wherefore the verses were couched in ambiguous terms that allowed for the foregone conclusions of the political powers. In other words, they believe the oracle was rigged: the pythia shrieked and the "gambler" or inquirer did whatever he and his faction back home planned on doing all along.

Trivia and Trivium

I have already discussed the goddess Trivia in my essay 'The Goddess Trivia'. She is the goddess of the crossroads or "three ways." She is also known as Hecate, a goddess very popular with those ancient Greek women who did not have much of a public life but who had their private ways, wiles, spells, charms and so on. Hecate is the goddess of witchcraft, sometimes depicted as the Terrible Mother. The Terrible Mother (made terrible by men) appeared in India as Kali, for example. Kali was worshiped by the murderous Thugs of India who posed as friendly fellow travelers in order to suddenly strangle their new companions of their worldly possessions. Parenthetically speaking here, no goddess-bashing is intended by the foregoing remarks. Since everyone is born of woman, she tends to get the blame when things go awry. Indeed, women themselves, in self-defense, contribute to the Terrible Mother myths: men had better beware of the invisible powers they are unconscious of!

The public crossroads can be dangerous places anywhere in the world, especially at certain times of night, but they do offer certain advantages as communication centers during daylight hours. Yes, some mothers may have been terrible to their sons after being regularly chastised by their spouses to keep them chaste, but the mothers, perhaps because of the so-called maternal instinct, loved their sons too and provided them with an early education in human discourse. In that sense mothers are communication centers, just as the Delphic oracle was a communication center of the Greek world.

I speak here of the mother as the first grammarian, the mother or Ma (measure) of language. She is of the Tree of Life, the first and last cross of man, the ark of life over time and space—incidentally, the cross used for crucifixions was once called a "hecate." She is where men first meet the world, the first trivium.

When the poorer children (mostly sons) went forth from their mothers for an ancient public education, they met at the public crossroads called a trivium (where three roads meet). Teachers who could not afford to rent a classroom sat up school at the trivium: it was a noisy dirty, distracting place to study, but the tuition was quite reasonable. The three R's were taught, yet the eventual emphasis was on what came to called the trivium: grammar, rhetoric, and dialectics. So the trivium was taught at the trivium, where sometimes the goddess Trivia was placed. The trivium is an intellectual or spiritual crossroads where neutral and good and evil meet to resolve their differences one way or another, hopefully according to the trivium instead of war. Even today, we find that those who master the world are masters of the trivium.

The Dragon and Three Paths

I must now be so vain again as to quote my muttering: "Where the three paths divide and migrate from their origin, where the decision tree first branches off in two directions no matter from what direction it is approached, ambiguity presides, there, in the streaming flux, by the cave where the dragon sleeps. "

The decision tree has three branches here, not four. As a crossroads, it is a trivium, not a quadrivium (the pedagogical quadrivium is the last four of the Seven Liberal Arts: arithmetic, geometry, astronomy, music). When man goes forward in time, he is faced with decisions: he has the power to decide and, condemned to freedom, he must decide—even his refusal to decide is a decision. In a manner of speaking, he is a condemned criminal because, to the extent he exists as an individual human, he would break the natural law as it is given. I mean the law of predictability, the law of regular cycles, the law of cause and effect, the law of death after life.

Man as such is a law unto himself, he has a free will, he is unpredictable, capable of arbitrary action. But he is not unlimited Power, or the God he would like to be. Man's freedom is that of a disobedient slave, for his very opposition to the world is the cause of his freedom and his existence as an individual human being.

Without that master shaping his resistance, man is not man: he is un-self-conscious, in total obedience, or dead. As resistance, the world is for man.

The ultimate biological limit is death by natural law. Man can use his freedom or power of decision, using the knowledge acquired to forestall that death, but he will ultimately fail by that means alone. Hence he is crucified on the Tree of Knowledge, the decision tree.

Still, man has recourse to himself by self-intercourse. Men and women are crucified in each others arms that they may be succeeded therefore succeed by succession: such is the Tree of Life. Here we see two serpents or dragons entwined about the Tao. We may also see the "Y", the "robber's cross" where life is given, to be taken away on the sides. If you prefer the Tau cross or "T", so be it.

Of course everyone is familiar with the prevarications we use to explain mysteries, and everyone can freely concoct their own, so I will not dwell on and of them at length here. I simply want to provide sufficient food for thought to elaborate the allusions made in my muttering. Yes, I should mention here that, besides the Tree of Life and Tree of Knowledge, there is the Tree of Heaven. I refer to the Celestial or Universal Tree whose fruits are the heavenly bodies existential and transcendental. In the trunk of this tree is hidden the Mystery of how and why God, who is unlimited Power, can be crucified in the flesh, or how in the world a universal can reside in one of its particulars.

Now then, I have referred to three trees. Each has three branches or three paths. The first paragraph of my essay on dragon sexuality, the muttering here discussed, mentions only the decision tree or Tree of Knowledge. I briefly mentioned the other two trees because the three trees are really one tree, and the three paths or branches of that one tree or cross are of one Substance emanating from its point of origin.

The mystery of that Substance or ultimate universal can only be illustrated and demonstrated by the Grand Dragon. No one man can see the entire Grand Dragon and live. However, minor dragons do appear from time to time. They tend to remain hidden now because of a rash of dragon crucifixions in the West—dragons were literally speared to trees representing good/evil decision trees (dragons are more kindly treated in the East). Yet they will reappear, in different forms: they always do. Remember, a dragon can be slain, dismembered and buried, but each piece of rotting flesh (pytho: "I rot") will eventually give birth to yet another dragon.

CONCLUSION

I have done my best to interpret the first paragraph of my dragon sexuality essay, which I excised from a dragon sleeping deep within the Internet archives. Mind you, it is only one paragraph, a tiny morsel of the colossal totem. I leave you to your own conclusions pursuant to your taste. My own conclusion is as follows:

My "muttering", so called by a critic, is one of great substance.

Maya

Maya is a mighty touchy subject, difficult if not impossible to comprehend. "By his powers of maya, Indra goes around in many forms." The heroic warrior-god Indra was not the only god with mayic powers. He supplanted the magnificent *mayin*, Varuna, god of justice and order, the guardian of fertile waters who stood in the firmament and used his mayic power to measure out the earth with a measuring stick - estimated to be about a yard long. And the magnificent Indra himself would eventually be demoted to a relatively minor status within the pantheon.

The term '*maya*' is derived from '*ma*', meaning, to measure out, that which measures out and limits. Hence maya is the power of measurement. Man refers to his own mayic power with the term '*manu*' or 'man', meaning, he who measures out thought - a mother or mama measures out creation - her children. As Protagoras said, Man is the measure of all things, those that are, that they are, those that are not, that they are not; but Protagoras did *not* mean that subjective individuals are *mayins* or that man is the creator of the objective universe. The meaning of abstract *maya* is threefold: in *maya* we have a trinity: creative power, creating, creation. That is, the Maker, Making, Made. Or, Cause, Force, Effect.

Now we recall that some time after Varuna measured out the creation, Vrita the river-dragon had a considerable power of his own - the power of envelopment. Vrita seized the fertile rivers from their guardian Varuna and holed up with the treasure in his ninety-nine fortresses. Indra - properly known as the truth that makes the knowers of it immune from punishment no matter what they do - got drunk on *soma* and slew Vrita with a thunderbolt. Wherefore the just and sometimes merciful Varuna was demoted because he had failed to personally keep the rivers within their beds. Varuna - a white man in golden armor seen riding a sea-monster and carrying snake-lasso - would henceforth be a sort of watchman over the rivers and oceans, while Indra lorded it over the creation. Indra would eventually have to make way for Visnu and Siva - Indra was demoted to preside over lesser gods and over the weather.

Individual men have reason to believe that they own *maya* and are therefore able to craft creation as they wish. On second thought, we have sufficient cause to believe that *maya* is not possessed by men but that men are possessed by maya. Indeed, Maya's fools are infinite in number. Even wise men have died in vain attempts to define *maya*. Just last week, two sages were mortally wounded when their dispute over *maya*'s true nature came to blows. They had agreed, first of all, that *maya* was god's power, and that it was indescribable. But then they tried to describe it, and got into a heated argument over whether or not maya can be terminated by right knowledge; whether or not it has a beginning; whether or not it both projects and veils the universe; whether or not it is the nature of existence; whether it is in the individual or the absolute or in both. And finally, they disagreed on their premise, that *maya* is indescribable, and went after each other with scissors.

Since all men and women are born of woman, woman originally gets the blame for such madness. The original mayas were *gnas*, the celestial wives of the gods. Abstractly speaking, *gna* is the feminine principle, a principle that is, according to the testimony of many men, far more deceptive than the male principle. Maya was first of all the cosmic mother and the world-goddess. Aristocratic mayas were the consorts of male gods. The ordinary maya is a temptress or feared woman. A woman who really knows her maya turn a warrior into a pussycat and have him eating out of her hand. In the Mahabhrata, the god uses his *maya* to delude mankind, to play with people as if they were toys. Of course women alone not to mention Venus are not really to blame for *maya*, the illusory, beguiling power, although their natural difference gives them cause to master it. Men of course have a hand in their own illusions and delusions - they are self-deluded to some extent. The erotic power makes two tangle. We are better off blaming our own ignorance than *maya*. Incidentally, according to some schools of thought, *maya* is a synonym for ignorance (*ajnana* and nescience (*avidya*).

Perhaps it is ignorance that leads men to believe that ignorance is caused by a certain and deliberate power, a divine power with two faculties: to project the world (*viksepa*), and cover or hide the truth (*avarana*). Some *fakirs* claim that this world is the one-god's sport or play because god has a whim to be many instead of one; those of us who are many are bewildered as a consequence of the projected divisions of the one; the truth is hidden by a cosmic veil; only a few *fakirs* can pierce that veil and be liberated from this illusory grinding up of the one - we can thank god that they might choose to stay behind and lead the rest of us out of our confusion. If only we really understood that the apparent multiplicity of our world is '*maya*' - our ignorance and illusion - the unreality negating the one true reality - we could cast off nature-ignorance, the mass delusion of the space-time continuum, and reside in blissful truth. How that bliss differs from death or nothingness is subject to further speculation.

With the advent of modern science, the term '*maya*' is most often employed in reference to feats of magic and illusionism. That is not to say that the prehistoric superstition attributing changes to the magical power of deities instead of natural forces has been extinguished in the popular mind. A secret *mayic* cult in Manhattan limits admission to applicants who can jump through a plate glass door without breaking the glass.

Sri Tundraputa claims they are wasting plate glass, for anyone possessed of the yogic powers can, for example, transform themselves into a subatomic particle, race though the earth and come out the other side with the greatest of ease. The plate glass is an illusion, he says, but it is a real illusion, and should not be bothered with as such. He pointed out that although the oldest scripture in the world, the *Rig-Veda*, sings of the power of deities to change shape and create illusory effects, nowhere do the Vedas question the reality of the illusory forms, no matter how incomprehensible those forms seemed at the time.

"*Maya* is the real cause of the material world," insisted Tundraputa. "*Maya* is just another name for Siva's guided energy, Sakti, or the mula-prakriti evolving as the phenomenal universe. Existence is necessarily restrained by *maya*. Time restrains eternity, hence we have mortality. Space restrains omnipresence, thus we have individuality. Desire restrains perfection; consequently, we have incessant activity and suffering. Learning limits omniscience, therefore our ignorance. Dependence limits omnipotence, fatality is the result. Our relation to the Lord is restrained by limitations obscuring the Lord. The Lord's creation is especially obscure for those Westerners whose knowledge is limited by subject-predicate linguistics and the logical subject-object or experiencer-experienced static dichotomy. Jumping through plate glass windows might get disillusioned kids into hospitals and mental wards, but they will soon be disillusioned with disillusionment or enslaved by insanity, an unwholesome liberation."

High Priestess Seized!

Those of us who have had our fortune told from time to time usually find out the hard way that oracles are unreliable or ambiguous. A particular reading can have so many different meanings that it could be applicable to almost anyone at any time, hence each person believes it is ready-made for him. Even a negative reading of, say, impending Death, can be interpreted positively in order to avoid it, perhaps by moving elsewhere; alas, Death is waiting elsewhere too, for everyone dies. And when the outcome is not the future event longed for, the fault is said not to be with the oracle as delivered in the dice cast, shuffled cards, or hysterical utterance of the Pythia at Delphi, but with the mistaken interpretation. The god Chance is never wrong: the fault resides in the priest or supplicant; and, when the random result seems too egregious to blame on its hapless victims, well, god works his will in mysterious ways, in ways contrary to the individual's will

Take for example the case of General Philomelus. He was chosen by the Phocians in about 357 B.C. to take possession of Apollo's temple at Delphi. The Amphictyonic assembly, an ancient Greek version of our United Nations with the rudimentary faults of same, was manipulated by Thebes to impose a huge fine on its neighbor Phocia due to charges brought on one pretext or another. As if the fine were not enough to resolve the Theban's ancient animosity over running border disputes, the assembly consecrated Phocian land to Apollo and declared the temple of Delphi thereon, then in possession of the Phocian's old brothers the Delphians, as the rightful possession of the Delphians.

Of course the Phocians were deeply offended by the assembly's sentence. Land consecrated to Apollo cannot be cultivated, hence the rug would be ripped right out from under them. According to one account, the huge fine was imposed for their cultivation of a rather small strip of land previously consecrated to Apollo. As for the temple of Apollo at Delphi, the very center of the Greek world, along with its function as an international gambling hall where outcomes were undoubtedly fixed in advance by the powers that be, its management belonged to the Phocians by right of ancient privilege recorded by Homer—the temple had been expropriated from the Phocians nearly eighty years prior to this present occasion for yet another "Sacred War."

General Philomelus lost no time raising funds, patriots, and mercenaries for the Sacred War. He attacked the town and temple of Delphi, capturing them both, then made himself master of the countryside. He proclaimed to the high heavens the ancient Phocian right to administer the temple, and he assured everyone concerned that the temple's treasures were in his safe hands. Thus in one stroke Philomelus had saved the sacred political casino and holy bank. However, something more spiritual was needed to make it official, namely, the rendering of the oracle in favor of his divine cause. Therefore he ordered the Pythian priestess to mount her tripod, the three-legged gambling bowl that had become the Pythia's sacred seat, and commanded her to deliver the desired oracle. I shall quote two of my favorite historians regarding this event: Diodorus of Sicily (1st century A.D.), a utilitarian whose work survived the centuries because it is a compendium of facts instead of voluminous fancy talk and theories; and George Grote (1794-1871), whose History of Greece is one of the great masterpieces of historical scholarship—he has fleshed out the old accounts of the event for our edification.

"When Philomelus had control of the oracle he directed the Pythia to make her prophecies from the tripod in ancestral fashion. But when she replied that such was not the ancestral fashion, he threatened her harshly and compelled her to mount the tripod. Then when she frankly declared, referring to the superior power of the man who was resorting to violence: 'It is in your power to do as you please,' he gladly accepted her utterance and declared that he had the oracle which suited him. He immediately had the oracle inscribed and set it up in full view, and made it clear to everyone that the god gave him the authority to do as he pleased. Having put together and assembly and disclosed the prophecy to the multitude and urged them to be of good cheer, he turned to the business of war." (Diodorus)

"Philomelus, while taking pains to set himself right in the eyes of Greece, tried to keep the prophetic agency of the temple in its ordinary working, so as to meet the exigencies of sacrificers and inquirers as before. He required the Pythian priestess to mount the tripod, submit herself to the prophetic inspiration, and pronounce the word thus put into her mouth, as usual. But the priestess—chosen by the Delphians, and probably herself a member of one among the sacred Delphian Gentes—obstinately refused to obey him; especially as the first question which he addressed concerning his own usurpation, and his chances of success against enemies. On his injunctions, that she should prophecy according to the traditional rites—she replied, that these rites were precisely what he had just overthrown; upon which he laid ahold of her, and attempted to place her on the tripod by force. Subdued and frightened for her own personal safety, the priestess exclaimed involuntarily that he might do as he chose. Philomelus gladly took this as an answer favorable to his purpose. He caused it to be put in writing and proclaimed, as an oracle from the god, sanctioning and licensing his designs. He convened a special meeting of his partisans and the Delphians generally, wherein appeal was made to this encouraging answer, as warranting full confidence with reference to the impending war. So it was construed by all around, and confirmatory evidence was derived from further signs and omens occurring at the moment. It is probably however that Philomelus took care for the future to name a new priestess, more favorable to his interest, and disposed to deliver oracular answers under the new administrators in the same manner as under the old." (Grote)

General Philomelus, thus favored by the oracle, went about the war and had some brilliant victories such as that against the Locrians. The Thebans, alarmed by that success, proceeded to organized the Amphictyonic states for an assault on Phocia "to assist the god." (Grote). Philolemus knew his only chance was to hire mercenaries to help him protect the god from the enemies who wanted to assist the god, so he most reluctantly borrowed some treasure from Apollo's vaults at the temple. His forces were given a fifty-percent raise, and there was the usual enrichment of friends and the adorning of wives with precious ornaments and fineries.

Despite the funds so impiously borrowed by the Phocians to increase their forces and the beauty of their women, the Thebans grew more and more confident of their success as the war drug on: so confident that, at one point in the conflict, they had all prisoners executed; the Phocians, not to be outdone, did likewise. To make a long story short, Philomelus eventually got his army into a bad position near the town of Neon:

"An engagement took place, and then a sharp battle in which the Boeotians (Thebans), who far outnumbered the Phocians, defeated them. As the flight took place through precipitous and almost impassable country many of the Phocians and their mercenaries were cut down. Philomelus, after he had fought courageously and had suffered many wounds, was driven into a precipitous area and there hemmed in, and since there was no exit from it and he feared the torture after capture, he hurled himself over the cliff and having made atonement to the god ended his life." (Diodorus)

Thus concludes the story of the general who seized the priestess at Delphi who then delivered the oracle that he could do as he pleased.

Whether he did his will or the god's will, or whether or not there is a difference between the two, we shall leave to the philosophers to settle.

Prelude to and Aftermath of The Sacred War

Circa 355 B.C.

The Amphictyonic ("dwellers around") league was an ancient and venerable Hellenic assembly of 12 nations of Northern Greece, fractions of the Hellenic name, associated to worship Apollo at Delphi and Demeter at Thermopylae. The original nations were the Thessalians, Boeotians, Dorians, Ionians, Perrhaebians, Magnetes, Lokrians, Aenians, Malians, Dolopians, Acheans and Phocians. Each nation had two votes regardless of its size. Its deputies were called Hieromnemones and Pylagorae. The assembly met twice annually, at Delphi in spring, and at Thermopylae in autumn.

Every fourth year, the assembly presided over the Pythian games at Delphi. The hero-worship at Delphi was tantamount to the papacy"s canonization of saints. Although the priests at Delphi soon complained that the rising popularity of sports and the glorification of athletes was a great evil leading to national ruin, the National Games did serve to bind the Greeks together, providing them with common ground whereupon individuals could prove their merit and virtue; furthermore, the prize competition of those dramatic poets who extolled the virtues of the heroes at the games led to the rise of Greek tragedy and comedy.

The Amphictyonic assembly was the legal guardian of the temple at Delphi, then considered to be the physical and spiritual center of the Greek world. There were numerous sacred wars for the honor of presiding over the temple, of which four were brought about by the assembly, ostensibly to protect the temple against the Crisaens (B.C.595), the Phocians (B.C. 355), the Amphissaeans (B.C. 340), and the Aetolians (B.C. 280).

Any dispute over the presidency of the temple threatened to ruin the Hellenic peace. There had been a tug of war over the site ever since it had become the center of the world. Apollo himself had reputedly seized the Egg guarded by Pytho the dragon, slaying the dragon and letting her rot there—hence the term 'Pytho' (I rot), and 'Pythia', the name of the woman or nun—probably of a Cretan order—whom the priests eventually allowed to sit on the tripod. We should note that Pytho was a dragoness until male poets provided her with a literary sex change, making a male of her. She was, in a manner of speaking, the Uterus guarding the World-Egg: the globular stone Omphalos found at the temple by which stood two golden effigies of the two eagles Zeus sent from East and West to meet at the Center of the World.

But there is another story of a more peaceable transaction, an economic transaction by which Apollo came into possession of the temple. The title to same had passed naturally, from Gaea, goddess of Earth, the daughter of Chaos, to her daughter Themis, goddess of law and prophecy—therefore no male was originally required to bring order to Earth. The Python dragoness was produced by Gaea to babysit her youngest son by Tartarus, Typhon, the giant hundred-headed beast symbolizing fire and smoke in the center of the Earth. Gaea, according to this economic account, shared Delphi with Poseidon, god of water, who gave his share to Apollo in exchange for the island of Calauria, subsequent to Themis transferring her inherited share to Apollo.

As for the evolution of the myth of Apollo, long before he became associated with the Sun or Light, he was a prehistoric Hercules, a heroic cave man, a wolf-god, then a shepherd-god who eventually immigrated to the city where he lived in a cave in the suburbs: thus he is the Traveler, the god of immigration. Therefore the concern at Delphi with colonization and constitutions, and the practice of sending out slaves tithed to the temple as immigrants to the colonies. In any event, no-one was to interfere with any colony sanctioned by Delphi.

The Delphian temple is located in Phocis (now within the Fokis Department) on the slope of Parnassus, about 6 miles from the Gulf of Corinth. Phocis gets its name from a mythological hero named Phocus, a descendant of Sisyphus, king of Corinth; Phocus inherited Phocia from his father Oryntus, who won it in a war from the Locrians; at least that is the story according to one of several real estate records.

Phocis was originally populated by the Aeolians. Some time prior to the 6th century B.C., Boeotians and Thessalians encroached and intermixed with the natives. The Delphians were originally of the Phocians name; and the Phocians were in possession of the famous temple at Delphi. One of the early disputes over that property both material and spiritual arose from the animosity of pilgrims who were being charged excessive tolls on the road through Crissa to Delphi; hence a coalition proclaimed (B.C. 590) a sacred war, destroyed Crissa and put the temple under a joint council.

Since international law was based on religious custom in those days, the Amphictyonic assembly had rather loosely defined political functions: it arbitrated conflicts between weaker states; imposed fines for illegal seizures of territory; protected water rights; prohibited the destruction of towns; and so on. It rarely meddled in the internal affairs of nations until the humiliation of Sparta by the Thebans at Leuktra (B.C. 371); thereafter, the Thebans proceeded to use the assembly for abusive political purposes, making of it the source of a great deal of mischief.

The Thebans brought suit before the assembly against defeated Sparta for seizing Cadmea (citadel of Thebes). A stiff fine was assessed and was doubled when the Spartans refused to pay it.

Although the Spartans had usually favored Delphian possession of the temple at Delphi, the assembly's judgment against the Spartans eventually prompted them to join the Phocians nearly sixteen years later during the nine-year Sacred War (B.C. 355) over Delphi, for the Spartans were still under burden of the huge indemnity imposed by the assembly after Leuktra. Since the temple at Delphi was the symbol of Greek unity, the question of who had the prestige of presiding over the temple and its treasures was of enormous political significance regardless of the small political power of the priesthood there, who tended to side with the apparently stronger military force and to conserve the foregone political conclusions given to them; in other words, the priests relied more on probability than chance to pick the winners and get on their good side.

The Phocians were traditionally the border-enemies of Thebes; in the war leading up to the defeat at Leuktra (B.C. 371), the Phocians had allied themselves with the Spartans against Thebes until submitting to Thebes after the battle of Leuktra; whereupon they formed and then broke off an alliance with same: they fought with the Thebans in the Peloponnese, but were negligent at the battle of Mantinea (B.C. 362). Miffed by the breach of promise, the Thebans brought a complaint before the Amphictyonic assembly against the Phocians on one pretext or another; we are not sure of which. According to one report, the grounds for complaint was that the Phocians had cultivated Cirrhaean, consecrated territory near Delphi on the Corinthian Gulf—land consecrated to Apollo was supposed to remain uncultivated, or conserved for the god. Another witness said the Phocians were charged with invading Boeotia without cause. Another report had them accused of carrying off a married Theban woman named Theano. Whatever the alleged offense, Thebes obtained a conviction. As in the case of the Spartans, a large fine was imposed. Furthermore, the assembly rendered a judgment recorded in a resolution engraved on a column at the Delphian temple, officially expropriating the temple from the Phocians and consecrating Phocian territory to Apollo.

The Phocians, under command of General Philomelus, rebelled against the assembly's incursion on their liberty and property, claiming they were the legitimate administrators of the temple by virtue of ancient privilege. As I have previously mentioned, Delphi was once a part of the Phocian name; according to the Homeric Catalogue, the Phocians had commanded "rocky Pytho" (Delphi) in the old days. And despite disputes and periods of joint management, the temple was in fact under Phocian control as late as 450 B.C. However, after a sacred war, with Phocians and Athenians on the one side, and Delphians, Spartans and Thebans on the other, the Phocians, because of the weakening of their allies the Athenians, relinquished control to the Delphians; hence the Delphians, severed from their Phocian brothers, assumed the lucrative business of the temple as formally confirmed by an article of peace in 421 B.C.

Nevertheless, the Phocians never gave up their claim to the administration of the temple at Delphi, a claim they vigorously pressed (B.C. 355) after being condemned by the Amphictyonic assembly at the Thebans' behest. In the ensuing nine-year Sacred War between Phocia and Thebes, on the side of the Phocians were Athens, Sparta , Peloponnesian Acheans, and some other Peloponnesian states; and on the side of the Thebans were the Thessalians and all the states north of Boeotia (Thebes was the principal city of Boeotia).

After General Philomelus was cornered and hurled himself to his death to escape torture, General Onomarchus took command of the war against Thebes and her allies; he was a despot who had no scruples about seizing whatever funds he needed from the temple and executing anyone who resisted or begged to differ. At the head of a formidable army of patriots and mercenaries, he won many battles and pressed as far north as Thermopylae, becoming its master; he also invaded Boeotia.

The Thebans were running out of money fast and were hard pressed to continue the war. Yet they were not the only ones who were short of funds: Onamarchus had nearly exhausted the holy coffers of their sacred money, and his allies the Athenians, who were also engaged in an antisocial Social War with their own allies at the same time as the Sacred War, were left empty-handed by the overdrawn account at Delphi. To compound adversity, Philip of Macedonia was up to his usual duplicitous machinations, posing a serious northern threat to Athens, hence she made overtures to Thebes for the sake of mutual protection. Philip, seeing that a general Hellenic peace would thwart his grand designs, made an overture to Athens; which she joyfully accepted despite the prescient warnings of her great speaker Demosthenes and others who foresaw the danger of an alliance to her independence.

After the deal was sealed, Philip marched through Thermopylae and right into Phocia. The Phocians, bereft of her Athenian allies, surrendered unconditionally. Philip occupied Delphi, took Phocia's two votes in the Amphictyonic assembly for himself, then had the assembly decree the destruction of all cities in Phocis (except Abae), their inhabitants were scattered into villages of not more than fifty houses each. Then the defender of the great god savior of his temple, Philip, together with the Thebans and Thessalians, presided over the Pythian games of B.C. 346.

Demosthenes, who rose from his speech disabilities to be one of the greatest speakers of all time, was right about Philip. Philip proceeded with his grand plans to attack Athenian cities, colonies and Persia. Athens combined with Thebes in defense, and their army met Macedonian forces on the plain of Chaeronea (B.C. 338). The Greeks were routed; Greece was crushed, becoming a mere province of Macedonia. Philip was kind to the defeated Athenians because of the love he acquired for Athens while living there for a couple of years during his younger days; but he was harsh to the defeated Thebans.

At a marriage festival in honor of his son Alexander the Great, Philip was assassinated (B.C 336) by a young man with a grudge who had concealed a long sword under his garment.

Alexander followed gloriously in his father's footsteps to his own grand destiny.

Note:

All dates given above are approximate

References:

Diodorus, Siculus, *Diodorus of Sicily*, Trans. Charles L. Sherman, Cambridge: Harvard

University Press, MCMLII

Grote, George, *History of Greece* (1846)

Pharaoh Alexander at Siwa Oasis

Alexander like other enterprising peacemakers before him was quite fond of oracles, wherefore, after being declared Pharaoh at Memphis, he went out of his way to the Siwa Oasis in Egypt to consult the oracle of ram-headed Ammon, whom the Greeks identified with Zeus – note that dissenting scholars insist that the Greeks clearly distinguished the Egyptian Ammon from the Greek Zeus.

Many reasons are supposed for Alexander's arduous trek into western Egypt to a temple where no Pharaoh had gone before. The way thereto was always beset with curious travails. Aristotle's pupil certainly did not associate the Delphic injunction, "Know Thyself", with a diminutive humble self defined by immediate circumstances. Quite to the contrary: he made a career of going way out of the way to extend himself, and his empire to boot.

Perhaps Pharaoh Alexander wanted to firmly establish his dominion on the Carthaginian frontier. Furthermore, it has been speculatively noted that he wanted to outdo his heroic ancestors, Perseus and Heracles, who had visited the god before him. Cato the true conservative would make a visit some time thereafter, before his famed Stoic suicide. Indeed, a visit to the temple should be included in any self-respecting poet's standard odyssey. Yet critical authors were quick to point out that a universal god is everywhere; besides, Zeus would not be such a fool as to place his temple in the middle of nowhere, making it exceedingly difficult for anyone to worship him.

Some say Alexander was told during his youth that Zeus was his ideal father, hence now he wanted divine verification. Not that he disrespected his real father, Phillip. The priest at Siwa greeted him as the "son of Ammon" - of course all pharaohs are by nature sons of God. Most likely he wanted confirmation of his fondest dream of all, that of successful conquest. However that may be, the priests took the egg-shaped idol from the inner sanctum and paraded it around the temple in its sacred arc or boat. In the procession the priests were by chance moved to turn this way and that, and the motions were in turn interpreted.

Alexander must have received the answer he craved. He kept it secret - and methinks he was wise to do so, knowing how critics love to bring positive mental attitudes to ruin. Thus he continued along the royal road of fame and fortune, with either his fortune or his godliness, or perhaps both, well assured.

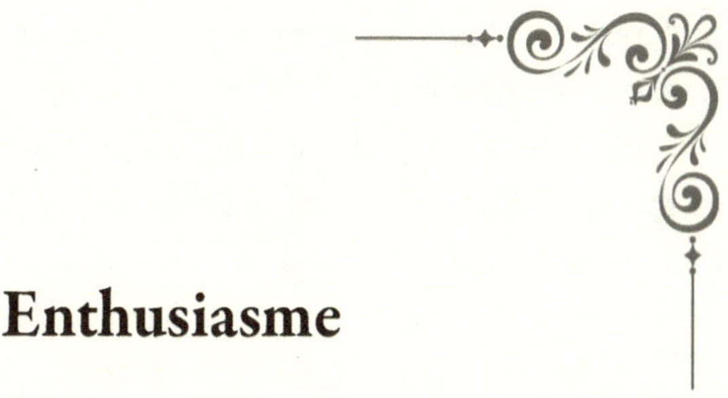

Enthusiasme

Florence Etienne Meric Casaubon (1599-1671) wrote a popular book entitled A TREATISE CONCERNING ENTHUSIASME as It is an Effect of Nature: but is mistaken by many for either Divine Inspiration, or Diabolical Possession, London: Roger Daniel, 1656, still appreciated to this day because of the author's Classical scholarship and firsthand experience with enthusiasm.

Meric's famous father, Isaac Casaubon (1559-1614), a fine French Classical scholar, had been educated at home by his own father, a pastor of the Reformed Church. Isaac studied at the Academy of Geneva, where he became Professor of Greek (1592-1596), and then he taught at Montpelier for awhile. He was denied a professor's chair at College Royal when he refused to convert to Catholicism after being called to the court of France, but he was still appointed an assistant in the king's library in 1604.

Isaac relocated to England in 1610 at the invitation of the Archbishop of Canterbury when Meric was scarcely eleven-years old. The after-effects of the Reformation wars were still being felt there as well as on the continent. Isaac was warmly welcomed by King James I, but he was hated by the enthusiastic Puritans until he died in 1614, when Meric was only fourteen.

Meric defended his father's religious views from Catholic calumnies in the years prior to taking his M.A. in 1621, favorably impressing the king. He wrote of the fanatic religious persecution of his Huguenot parents and grandparents. He was living on church preferments when they were suspended around 1644, and he was said to have been jailed for awhile. He had refused to recognize Cromwell's authority, yet Cromwell offered him a commission to write a history of the Civil War, which he politely declined, but Cromwell was not thereby offended and tried to anonymously donate money to him, which Meric did not take. He managed to steer clear of serious trouble during the troubled times. He witnessed the general turmoil and religious-political squabbles that resulted in the Civil War of 1642-1646, the Second Civil War in 1648, the beheading of Charles I in 1649, and Cromwell designated Lord Protector (1653-1658). Charles II was proclaimed king in 1660; Cromwell's body was dug up and hung, much to the relief of people who were sick and tired of Puritan enthusiasm not to mention the enthusiasm of Ranters, Fifth Monarchy Men, Seekers, Quakers, and damning Muggletonians.

Meric's preferments were restored, and his second wife had a fortune. He devoted himself to literary pursuits. He took a dim view of the various strains of enthusiasm or "god-possession" that he had seen. Being the good Classicist that he was, he used the authority of the ancients to broaden the modern view of his subject and to justify his own position, which was, in short, that genuine powers of divination or god-possession indeed exist, providing the source of inspiration is the Christian god. Most enthusiasm, however, is due to mental disease, having, most probably, physical causes. He mentioned melancholia, mania, phrenia, epilepsy, and hysteria. He also believed that enthusiasm is feigned to take advantage of the credulity and superstition of people; therefore a scientific approach to enthusiasm is advisable.

He claimed that religious zeal is a harlequinade, a comedy whose protagonist is a buffoon. What is important is the truth of what is said, not how it is said. Moreover, he stated that the success of rhetoric is due to learned skill and long practice, not to enthusiasm. He therefore rejected the notion that the basis of art and literature is divine inspiration, and relates how facile speakers amazed auditors with their eloquence and reasoning, reason being perceived by ignorant hearers as divinely inspired. The reasoning power of logos evolved from crude beginnings, and his account of it confirms that it has been the cause of a great deal of dissension:

"In most things that they did, more guided by certain, sudden instincts and raptures, than by reason, not out of any contempt of it, but because they had it not. In those days there was no moral philosophy: and they were accounted worthy of highest honors that could utter most sentences that had somewhat of reason in them; which by other men were generally received as Oracles because they seemed to surpass the wisdom of ordinary men. There were as many Religions almost as men; for every man's religion was his fancy; and they had most credit and authority that could best invent, and make best show.

Among so many religions, there were no controversies, but very good agreement and concord; because no reason was used either to examine, or to disprove." He recounts the story of a man who could read from a book length, then put it down, close his eyes and continue the theme at length as if he were still reading from the book. And he wrote of Cicero's eloquent defense of a man Caesar had all ready decided to condemn:

"Caesar was so affected, that his very face suffering many changes in a little time, sufficiently betrayed the inward commotion of his soul: until at last, passion and amazement had so wholly possessed him, that his whole body began to tremble; so that be let some papers fall to the ground out of his hands, because he was not able to hold them, and in confusion, Cicero had no sooner done speaking, than Caesar, without any further deliberation, acquitted him for whom he had spoken."

Meric's arguments are hardly novel. His scholarship is impeccable. Like any good lawyer, he brings out the opposing views, before dismissing them before the Supreme Court, admitting to a few exceptionable cases of genuine enthusiasm, particularly that of Jesus the Christ and the Apostles. Anything less would be blasphemous! Not everyone can be directly inspired by the legitimate divinity. The Holy Spirit is made available to the priestly authority for distribution to us. Meric was certainly was not impressed by the Puritan fanatics or the Quakers of his day, who were shivering and shaking, interrupting sermons in their "meeting houses", gathering enthusiastic crowds in open fields and preaching direct communion with God.

Meric points out there were many cases of enthusiasm in ancient times. He mentions amongst others the pythias at Delphi, and the female Syrian prophets that Alexander an Marius took on their campaigns, and the case of the slave girl who was following Paul and company around in Macedonia (Acts 16), doing a divinatory business on the side for her masters until the demon was cast out of her.

"These (enthusiasts) were for the most part of the meanest sort of men, women often, neither so experienced in the world, or so perfected by study, as that any could perfect them to deal cunningly."

He admits to the sincerity of the mentally disturbed enthusiasts. Enthusiastic divinations are not always impostures designed to obtain money from gullible people, "or, at the best, the subtle devices of and artifices of well-meaning politicians to compass great matters for the good of the people." The histories indicate that enthusiasm was sincere in many cases, not simply feigned for ulterior motives. Again, the historical enthusiasts were mentally disturbed individuals who could have been treated and cured by medical methods known even to ancient physicians. As for those who feign enthusiasm:

"(We find) in the carriage of these things, much error and deceit, and perchance some particular places and Oracles, where all that outwardly had a show of Enthusiasm, was nothing but Art and Imposture. But that is as good to say that there is not truth in the world because there is nothing in the world that is not liable to the imposture of men."

He did not confine his studies to the religious character of enthusiasm according to its strictest definition (god-possessed). Following the Classical method of Plato and Plutarch, he derived therefrom five kinds of enthusiasm: "Divinatorie", "Contemplative" or "Philosophicall", "Rhetoricall", "Poeticall", and "Precatory" (praying). He gave due attention to the debased commercial, political, and literary enthusiasm of his day, coming down hard on the sophisticated rhetorical impostures. Still, since certain poets and other authors and orators claim to receive their inspiration from divine divinities, muses, and gods, from which they prophesy as to the future and to what is best for us, the divinatory is at the top of the list. He said of the Divinatory classification, that:

"Enthusiasm is most properly used to imply Divination, such as by inspiration. And because such Divination among Heathens was not usually without a temporary alienation of the mind, and distraction of the senses; hence it is that, both in Greek and in Latin, it is taken sometimes for deliration and idle speaking." And, "It is acknowledged, as well by Heathens as by Christians, that it is absolutely and infallibly to foretell things future, doth belong to him only, to whom all things passed, present, and future are equally present."

EXCERPTS:

A Treatise Concerning Enthusiasme, As it is an Effect of Nature: but is mistaken by many for either Divine Inspiration, or Diabolical Possession (1655):

"That which I have here to show, and to maintain, is, that the opinion of divine Inspiration, which in all ages, and among all men of all professions, Heathens and Christians, has been a very common opinion in the world; as it hath been common, so the occasion of so many evils and mischiefs among men, or delusion of what kind soever, hath been or been or either more, or greater. By the opinion of divine Inspiration, I mean a real, though but imaginary, apprehension of it in the parties, upon some ground of nature; a real, not barely pretended, counterfeit, and simulative, for political ends. For that hath ever been one of the main crafts and mysteries of government, which the best of heathens sometimes (as well as the worst, more frequently,) the most commended. Heroes, in ancient times, upon great attempts and designs, have been glad to use."

"In most things that they did, more guided by certain sudden instincts and raptures, than reason; not out of any contempt of it, but because they had it not. In those days there was no moral Philosophy: and they were accounted worthy of highest honors, that could utter most sentences that had somewhat of reason in them; which by other men were generally received as Oracles, because they seemed to surpass the wisdom of ordinary men. There was no talk among men, but of dreams, revelations, and apparitions: and they that could so easily fancy God in whatsoever they did fancy, had no reason to mistrust or to question the relations of others, though never so strange, which were so agreeable to their humors and dispositions; and by which themselves were confirmed in their own supposed Enthusiasms. That was the condition in those days, (in Greece at least, in those parts) as it is set out by ancient Historiographers, and others; until the days of Socrates, who for his innocent heroic life (commended and admired by Christians as well as Heathens) and his unjust death, (to which he was chiefly condemned for speaking against the Idolatry of his times) might be thought in some measure (as amongst Heathens) to have born the Image of Christ; but certainly without some mystery, and some preparation of men to Christianity, was so magnified by all men, for being the founder of moral Philosophy, and for bringing the rule of Reason into request: by which we would have all things tried, nor anything believed, or received upon any private account or authority, that should be against Reason. Logos was the word which he had so frequent in his mouth and which he so commended to his auditors and disciples: and Logos, though in a far different sense I know, is the world by which Christ is styled in the Gospel. And as it is commonly observed, and true, that at the coming of Christ or thereabouts, all Oracles in all parts of the world began to cease; so we may say that even of this somewhat might be prefigured in Socrates, by whose doctrine, as it did increase in the world, (as we know it did in a little time very mightily,) so private inspirations and Enthusiasms began to be out of request, and men became, as more rational everywhere in their discourse, so more civil in their conversations."

Dossier: Marguerite Porete, Love's Martyr

Letter to Lady Marguerite from David Arthur Walters

Most Courteous Lady,

As I scratch out this appeal for your transcendent charms, a brief glance over your heavenly shoulder would make of a instant a joyful epoch for me. Indeed, the mere reflection of your face in the mirror would repay my fond regard with the sweetest of countenances. Furthermore, for the bare image of your fleeting presence, I would rhapsodize the millenniums with songs praising your beauty. Although in your supreme modesty you may demur that you are less than nothing because you are oppressed by nothingness, your bounty is more than enough for me.

Please allow me to introduce myself. I am a man of substance who feels substantial discontent drawing lines frantically across pages from left to right, denying all conclusions, frightened by the possibility of a final period. I forsake the roman rhythm as well as the familiar habit of rhyming. I flee from the discipline of the stuffy old schools of vain, vapid repetitions which lend a smug feeling to what is really awfully *straunge.* Wherefore, Madame, I plead for your literal grace.

My poor writing hand is moved to form letter after letter, bid by some unseen but certain force to spell out my crude incantation invoking a precious glimpse of your illumined being eternally crowned by courage. Perchance I shall feel your gracious hand brush mine as

I stroll this incoherent ramble which impatiently awaits the elevating rapture to your transcendental realm of purest Love.

Dearest Lady, I have for too long been stumbling over the tombstones of times in places, terminals for the ever molting flesh marking off this world as a labyrinth of vanishing forms. Lovely though illusions may be, I am left alone, disillusioned, pending your gracious presence. Thus I foster a point of life in the void, a glowing spark from the bonfire of your humble spirit exalted at the Place de Greve and carried down to me by winds whispered through nunnery and monastery.

Many are your lovers, Lady, and many are those who fail to convey the beauty of your flame in words: even their best texts cloth your glory in a drab garment not quite gray or brown. Compared to those fashionable wordsmiths cluttering your court with their fancy ornaments, I bray, barely, like a donkey from the alley, yet still I venture to say that I love you more than any other.

Oh, Fond Lady, if only I possessed the fine phrases and melodies of a brash troubadour such as King Peire! Ah, but you are not deceived by the courtesies at your feet. Nor are you disturbed by the flesh ensouled, for you know a man's love for a lady is not altogether carnal - true love cannot be incorporated.

True lovers must confess, Lovely Lady, that lovers love most the Ideal Lady, although they see her not in the shimmering pool of their own vanity. The Ideal Lady is the mirror before whom each poor soul performs all those acts falling, like tears, tragically short of perfection. Nevertheless, finding himself alone after bitter experience, the hapless romantic wretch would once more sacrifice flesh to his consuming passion. Yet it is not passion that drives the lover mad, but the flesh, for the spirit makes him whole - the lover is mad in matter but sane in spirit. And there rests the fundamental hypocrisy, the ground of divorce and the fulsome motive for reconciliation.

By your most gracious leave, Joyous True Lady, permit me to mention King Peire again. I know his vanity and love for women in the flesh shall offend you not, for you are a playwright and poet on the highest stage of all. You fully fathom the extent of love - and deep in love you shall find me your most humble servant. Still, I am not as well versed and adept in these matters as Peire Vidal. Therefore, in closing, I faithfully recite a few of his words while praying that you shall accept the spirit of his text in my context, and respond to me anon.

"Nothing has pleased me so well as the Joyous True Lady
In whom is every good quality without any evil.
Since all things are in her that are fitting to love,
I am lucky if only I may be there,
And if mercy, which makes all good things to increase,
Avail me aught with her,
I may say without any denial
That I never could effect so much with love."
"Soon can she be overthrowing grief
If on one's heart it seizes
E'n the thought of her appeases woe,
And he whose praise is glowing never to speak false need fear
Surely she has no peer.
None so fair in mirror gazes."

Most Truly Yours,

David Arthur Walters

Abstract of Criminal Record

NAME: Marguerite Porete,

PROSECUTING AUTHORITY: the Inquisition, under Philip the Fair.

DATE OF ARREST: about 1308

PLACE OF RESIDENCE: Hainaut, a medieval county presently in N. France and S.W. Belgium

INFORMATION: brought forth by Guy II's successor, Philip of Marigny, Bishop of Cambrai, N. France, that the suspect was spreading heresy "among simple people and beghards." The case was referred to high authority, the Provincial Inquisitor of Haute Lorraine, N.E. France, then on to Paris.

FORMAL CHARGE: Heretical Mysticism. Marguerite elevated mystic Love over Reason in her latest book, arousing the sexual fears of the pious authorities and threatening the patriarchal structure of society based upon "male" reason. She had submitted her book for preliminary critical appraisal to three spiritual authorities: Friar Minor John de Querayn, a liberal, representative of the most modern movement; Cistercian Frank of the Abbey of Villiers, a conservative, exponent of the monastic traditions; Godfrey of Fontaines, famous theologian and scholastic, ex-regent of Paris University, a moderate. The critics said her work was legitimate, but two of them warned her not to publishing it.

DIVISION OF THE CHARGE: The formal charge was divided as follows:

1. The accused said that, via Seven Stages of Grace, the Soul is united with the Trinity in the Fifth and Sixth Stage, or God Himself, without any searching;

2, The accused said the Soul is liberated from the Virtues;

3. The accused said Love is the Great Church and that Reason is the Little Church;

4. The accused said the Soul does not seek God by Works, Thoughts, or

Words;

5. The accused said union with God is NOW and in THIS world, in this bodily existence;

6. The accused made her book public;

7. The accused refused to answer questions.

RELIGIOUS AFFILIATION: Suspected Beguine, a heretical, penitential secular order of women religious, originally appearing in the 12th century at Liege, Belgium.

PREVIOUS RECORD: Condemned for heresy by Guy II, Bishop of Cambrai. The book in question was burned in the public square of her then residence, Valenciennes, and its use was prohibited under pain of excommunication. She was released.

PLACE OF TRIAL AND EXECUTION: Paris. Marguerite Porete is believed to be the first heretic burned at Paris by the Inquisition.

PRESIDING: Master William Humbert of Paris, a Dominican, Inquisitor General of the Kingdom of France, King Philip's confessor. He had also presided over the trial of the Templars. Master William, reputedly a sinister man. According to one rumor, the trial and execution of Marguerite was token compensation to the Pope for the outrageous destruction of the Church's Knights Templars. The Beguines believed the Pope was the Antichrist, therefore prosecuting Marguerite as a Beguine would have demonstrated unwavering devotion to the Pope.

EXPERT WITNESSES: a special commission of 21 theologians from Paris University assembled at the Church of St.Mathurin. The accused's book was adjudged heretical by the commission based upon sections taken out of context. Note: Marguerite had on previous occasions called the Paris University theologians churls, merchants, small minds, sheep and asses.

EVIDENCE: Her book, *The Mirror of Simple Souls*, wherein she exalts mystic Love over Reason. After Marguerite was executed, the book circulated anonymously in monasteries and nunneries. It was eventually widely circulated in several languages, having a revolutionary influence on spiritual thinking. The book was not attributed to Marguerite of Hainaut until 1946 (by Romana

Guarnieri). It has been critically acclaimed as the finest work written in the Old French vernacular.

DEFENSE WITNESS: Beghard Guiard de Cressonessart, a Joachimist millenarian who was said to have the keys of David, therefore also known as the "Angel of Philadelphia," was disposed to testify in Marguerite's favor. He was arrested in 1308 by order of Master William and an effort was made to force him to testify on Marguerite's "behalf"; that is, for her "salvation". He was imprisoned for 18 months to reflect, then he refused to appear. Faced with the death penalty, he retracted his obstinate position and was condemned to life imprisonment.

MARGUERITE'S PERSONAL DEFENSE: After 18 month's imprisonment to reflect, Marguerite refused to appear, refused to swear to tell the "truth" to the Inquisitor, and refused to retract in the face of death.

VERDICT: Guilty as charged. Remanded to the civil authorities on May 31, 1310 as it was unconscionable for the Christian spiritual authorities to actually murder the people they condemned.

SENTENCE: Death. Marguerite was burned at the stake on June 1, 1310, at Place de Greve, now Place d l' Hotel de Ville. An enormous crowd attended and many were converted to her favor because of her courage at the stake. Those who love her say she was sacrificed not to the Pope but to Love.

Marguerite's Nine Points For Contemplation

1. The Soul cannot be found. The Soul is crushed by all it knows, its sins, which are really nothing, hence the "annihilated" Soul itself is less than nothing.

2. The Soul is saved by Faith and not by works. Faith imparts the Trinity, and one can do nothing of her own will.

3. The Soul is alone in Love. The Soul finds no comfort in any creature except God, therefore asks nothing of creatures.

4. The Soul does nothing for God. God has no use for works, and the Soul has use only for what God does. Since He is infinitely rich, she can never be poor.

5. The Soul leaves nothing aside that she can do for God. She does only the will of God, and never thinks against God.

6. The Soul can be taught nothing. The One she loves was never known and never will be, and is greater than all the knowledge in the world.

7. Nothing can be taken away from the Soul. God is not in possessions, and everything taken away from the Soul leaves God in her as God.

8. One can give the Soul nothing. What she has already exceeds anything that can be given. The "less" she has, the "more" God has in her.

9. The Soul has no will. God is her only will.

Summary: Pure Love allows the Soul to be abandoned to the annihilated life, becoming the fixed abode of Charity

The Beguines

The Beguine movement started during the 12th century in Belgium among upper-class women, then spread to middle-class women and eventually to poorer women.

Wealthy and noble medieval women were faced with the prospect of obtaining a husband or becoming cloistered in a convent. Since the dowries charged by convents were exorbitant, convents became havens for rich women, often served by poor women. The resulting disparity between rich and poor women in the cloisters caused reformers such as Clare of Assisi to work towards restoring the simple apostolic life to the convents.

To make matters worse, the ravages of war, disease and guild rules caused women in general to be faced with a shortage of men available for marriage. Feudal society was in the process of being disintegrated as the market economy symbolized by money grew; the nobility were selling land and titles; the powerless people (pauperese) or poor and unemployed were wandering the countryside. The social authorities were seeking a norm in contrast to the disruptions of the old order. They found deviates or social "lepers" to persecutes, such as Jews, sodomites, prostitutes, fools and so on, and natural allies in the rising merchant class. Medieval women did have their guilds - women virtually dominated the textile industry - yet they were faced with the hostility and lawsuits of the dominant all-male guilds.

Out of those conditions grew beguinages, or women's lodgings where a few-score women without husbands or access to convents would reside together for their own security and use their skills to provide services to the public such as weaving, nursing, and housework. The Beguines promised to remain chaste while residing at the beguinages, but could leave and marry at will. Their spiritual concerns were served by Dominican and Franciscan friars, natural allies to the impoverished pursuant to the example set by Francis of Assisi, the sainted hero of social "lepers". some of whom believed he was the promised Christ - as for real lepers, liberals were glad to kiss their sores for they lepers had fully suffered for man's sins hence were closest to God. Mysticism rapidly spread among the beguinages; with the advance of literacy, enthusiastic spiritual journals became quite the rage.

It is believed that the term Beguine derives from the French word "bege" (beige), or perhaps "baga" (hood), referring to the grey-brown homespun cloth St. Francis and other spirituals were fond of. The spiritual impact of St. Francis was tremendous during this crucial medieval period; in fact, it has been said that, if this early Reformation had succeeded, today's "Christians" would be calling themselves "Franciscans."

Joachim of Flora's writing was the spiritual movement's manifesto. Based on his studies of the Bible and the Trinity, Joachim concluded that there are three ages - Law, Faith, and Love - and that the Age of Love according to the Eternal Gospel was already upon the world, for which he proposed an ideal social order, namely, the monastic life. Joachim himself was not a revolutionary nor was he convicted of heresy, but reformers eagerly seized upon his Age-of-Love historical concept and concluded that the Age of Faith, meaning that of the Catholic Church, was over.

It was indeed a crucial time. The battle between God and Money was actually being fought out in the courts. The main question being tried was whether Jesus and the apostles held property individually, or in common, or neither. The Pope, who was not only powerful but an excellent lawyer, won the case for materialism with brilliant, sophisticated arguments.

Meanwhile, the counterparts to the Beguines, the mendicant Beghards, or beggars, were wandering about in the name of God; some of them, of course, accumulating quite a bad reputation along the way. A few wealthy men who took the Bible literally were caught up by the revival, gave their fortunes to beguinages and joined the Beghards. Thus the Beguine movement, in receiving both income and capital investment, was not only a spiritual but an economic threat to the Church.

JAROSLAV VRCHLICKY'S poetic interpretation of Joachim de Flora's "eternal gospel."

ETERNAL GOSPEL (1240)

Now what is written in the revelation will come to pass. Indeed, first of all a great morning will shine out for humanity. Again the Angel flies through the ravine over the abyss and he holds the eternal gospel so that he can announce it over the mountains and the waters into the crowd of the languages of all men and of all clans.

The world is sinking in the flood of vanity and blood.

Who sees the Angel as he flies through the dark skies? This heavenly guest is half hidden by stars; Down below the world sleeps or wallows in vices; The mitre weights heavily on pope, and on king weighs heavily the wreath, on scholar the book. At midnight my eyes rise to the sky.

Behold, the clasp of the book flashes in the clouds!

Here on a rocky slope in Calabria, where wolves vie with the wind in their howling; here I am close to the sky, and, indeed, I see it. And I let myself be guided by the words of the Apostle; Now we see everything as in a mirror! But withered leaves will rise again through new sap!

Oh, listen, you whose hearts are tired, have lost their warmth! Says the Angel of God, who flies above the world.

The only and the third Kingdom of the Spirit will come, when all riches and possessions and gold, jewels, base wealth will be mere mire, when the poor in goods will be rich in spirit, and the world comes alive with the bustle of eternal spring.

With trembling, joyous ear I listen to him.

He speaks in the wind; he speaks in the thunder; I know he tells the truth, for from one side here I look at Sodom and Rome, and from the other side I look in anger at Byzantium and Gomorrah, and I weigh up their error and guilt, and I do not wonder the world lies in shadows.

He rides into the world like a fiery wedge.

The kingdom of the Father has been: that was the flaring of sweet stars. The kingdom of the Son has been: that was the smiling of the Moon. The kingdom of the Spirit is to come, an unperishing Sun; I can hear the wings of its messengers beating... Those two kingdoms are past and the third is arising; its glory is already dawning in the East.

The Angel waves the great book over the world.

The kingdom of Laws, suffering and anxiety has been; the kingdom of mercy, Faith and discipline has been; now the kingdom of Love will come, the kingdom of eternal Love! You tarried only at the entrance of the sanctuary, but now you will yourselves enter the tabernacle; you will walk on roses, where you used to walk on nettles.

A 'Halleluja' sounds through the expanse of worlds.

Oh, all of you come to the one table! First there was the Bible, and the the Apostles' joy-giving message spread itself onto the drawn world. Now the eternal gospel transmits its glowing flame; now the true freedom of human souls will begin, the freedom which will victoriously trample all chains into the dust.

My vision suggests to me this kingdom of the Spirit.

Through that kingdom I hack myself out a way over the weir of eloquence. Francis will be its high priest; he will complete Christ in the future age, for Christ stooped only to man, where Francis stooped to animal, and took matter into his loving embrace.

Therefore he is the centre of the great third kingdom.

All that the Angel said to me in the dark night, as I was finishing the 'Ave' on my rosary and as I turned to gaze from the heights of Calabria into the darkness of the world, which is putrefying in injustices, on the one hand harnessed under the yoke of the she-wolf of Rome, on the other hand pursued by the hangmen of Byzantium:

I, Joachim of Fiore, prophecy this golden age.

SOURCE: Jaroslav Vrchlick Druha antologie z vasni Jar. Vrcklickeho (Prague: Otto, n.d. (1903) 'Vecne evangelium'. Jaroslav Vrchlicky's poem was set to music by composer Leos Janacek

(1854-1928) in his cantata, 'Eternal Gospel' (1914), reminiscent of a Glagolitic Mass. Vrchlicky was born in 1853. His real name was Emil Frida. He is often referred to as "the unknown father of Czech poetry." Besides his 85 volumes of lyric verse, Jaroslav Vrchlicky wrote 270 volumes translating world literature from French, Spanish, Italian, and German into his native tongue, in order to bring Czechoslovakia out of its provincial corner. Vrchlicky's poetry is epic, contemplative, lyric and philosophical. His favorite subjects were the Bible and Talmud, Greek and Roman reasoning, the Renaissance, Provence tales, sorcery, knighthood, geniuses, heretics, battles and wars. He was greatly influenced by Victor Hugo's stories of humanity's triumph over cruelty and fanaticism. He advocated using improvisational techniques for writing and living: "If life is good, the improvisations are good." He was inspired by his wife Sofi Podlipsaka, with whom he raised three children. In 1892 he received a letter informing him he was not the father of two of them - this was reportedly a cause of great despair to him. He died in 1912.

Christus: A Mystery - Henry Wadsworth Longfellow

First Interlude: the Abbot Joachim,
a room in the convent of Flora in Calabria, at night.)
Joachim:
The wind is rising; it seizes and shakes
The doors and window-blinds and makes
Mysterious moanings in the halls;
The convent-chimneys seem almost
The trumpets of some heavenly host,
Setting its watch upon our walls!
Where it listeth, there it bloweth;
We hear the sound, but no man knoweth
Whence it cometh or whither it goeth,
And thus it is with the Holy Ghost.
O breath of God! O my delight

In many a vigil of the night,
Like the great voice in Patmos heard
By John, the Evangelist of the Word,
I hear thee behind me saying: Write
In a book the things that thou hast seen,
The things that are, and that have been,
And the things that shall hereafter be!
This convent, on the rocky crest
Of the Calabrian hills, to me
A Patmos is wherein I rest;
While round about me like a sea
The white mists roll, and overflow
The world that lies unseen below
In darkness and in mystery.
Here in the Spirit, in the vast
Embrace of God's encircling arm,
Am I uplifted from all harm
The world seems something far away,
Something belonging to the Past,
A hostelry, a peasant's farm,
That lodged me for a night or day,
In which I care not to remain,
Nor, having left, to see again.
Thus, in the hollow of Gods hand
I dwelt on sacred Tabor's height,
When as a simple acolyte
I journeyed to the Holy Land,
A pilgrim for my master's sake,
And saw the Galilean Lake,
And walked through many a village street
That once had echoed to his feet.
There first I heard the great command,

The voice behind me saying: Write!
And suddenly my soul became
Illumined by a flash of flame,
That left imprinted on my thought
The image I in vain had sought,
And which forever shall remain;
As sometimes from these windows high,
Gazing at midnight on the sky
Black with a storm of wind and rain,
I have beheld a sudden glare
Of lightning lay the landscape bare,
With tower and town and hill and plain
Distinct and burnt into my brain,
Never to be effaced again!
And I have written. These volumes three,
The Apocalypse, the Harmony
Of the Sacred Scriptures, new and old,
And the Psalter with Ten Strings, enfold
Within their pages, all and each,
The Eternal Gospel that I teach.
Well I remember the Kingdom of Heaven
Hath been likened to a little leaven
Hidden in two measures of meal,
Until it leavened the whole mass;
So likewise will it come to pass
With the doctrines that I here conceal.
Open and manifest to me
The truth appears, and must be told;
All sacred mysteries are threefold;
Three Persons in the Trinity,
Three ages of Humanity,
And holy Scriptures likewise three,

Of Fear, of Wisdom, and of Love;
For Wisdom that begins in Fear
Endeth in Love; the atmosphere
In which the soul delights to be
And finds that perfect liberty
Which cometh only from above.
In the first Age, the early prime
And dawn of all historic time,
The Father reigned; and face to face
He spake with the primeval race.
Bright Angels, on his errands sent,
Sat with the patriarch in his tent;
His prophets thundered in the street;
His lightnings flashed, his hailstorms beat;
In earthquake and in flood and flame,
In tempest and in cloud He came!
The fear of God is in his Book;
The pages of the Pentateuch
Are full of the terror of his name.
Then reigned the Son; his Covenant
Was peace on earth, good-will to man;
With Him the reign of Law began.
He was the Wisdom and the Word,
And sent his Angels Ministrant,
Unterrified and undeterred,
To rescue souls forlorn and lost,
The troubled, tempted, tempest-tost
To heal, to comfort, and to teach.
The fiery tongues of Pentecost
His symbols were, that they should preach
In every form of human speech
From continent to continent.

He is the Light Divine, whose rays
Across the thousand years unspent
Shine through the darkness of our days,
And touch with their celestial fires
Our churches and our convent spires.
His Book is the New Testament.
These Ages now are of the Past;
And the Third Age begins at last.
The coming of the Holy Ghost,
The reign of Grace, the reign of Love
Brightens the mountain-tops above,
And the dark outline of the coast.
Already the whole land is white
With Convent walls, as if by night
A snow had fallen on hill and height!
Already from the streets and marts
Of town and traffic, and low cares,
Men climb the consecrated stairs
With weary feet, and bleeding hearts;
And leave the world and its delights,
Its passions, struggles, and despairs,
For contemplation and for prayers
In cloister-cells of cenobites.
Eternal benedictions rest
Upon thy name, Saint Benedict!
Founder of convents in the West,
Who built on Mount Cassino's crest
In the Land of Labor, thine eagle's nest!
May I be found not derelict
In aught of faith or godly fear,
If I have written, in many a page,
The Gospel of the coming age,

The Eternal Gospel men shall hear.
Oh may I live resembling thee,
And die at last as thou hast died;
So that hereafter men may see,
Within the choir, a form of air,
Standing with arms outstretched in prayer,
As one that hath been crucified!
My work is finished; I am strong
In faith and hope and charity;
For I have written the things I see,
The things that have been and shall be,
Conscious of right, nor fearing wrong;
Because I am in love with Love,
And the sole thing I hate is Hate;
For Hate is death; and Love is life,
A peace, a splendor from above;
And Hate, a never-ending strife,
A smoke, a blackness from the abyss
Where unclean serpents coil and hiss!
Love is the Holy Ghost within
Hate the unpardonable sin!
Who preaches otherwise than this
Betrays his Master with a kiss!

www.ingramcontent.com/pod-product-compliance
Lightning Source LLC
LaVergne TN
LVHW091058150826
845673LV00002B/634

* 9 7 9 8 2 3 0 7 4 9 4 1 7 *